THE ISLE OF SKYE

PHOTOGRAPHS BY
COLIN BAXTER

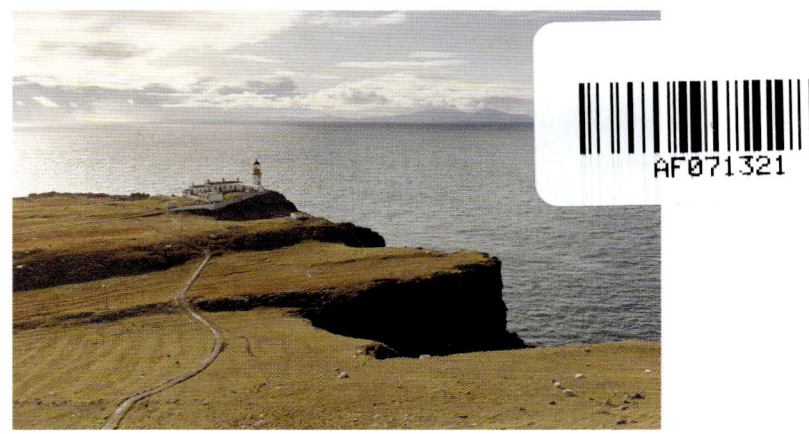

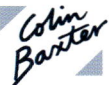

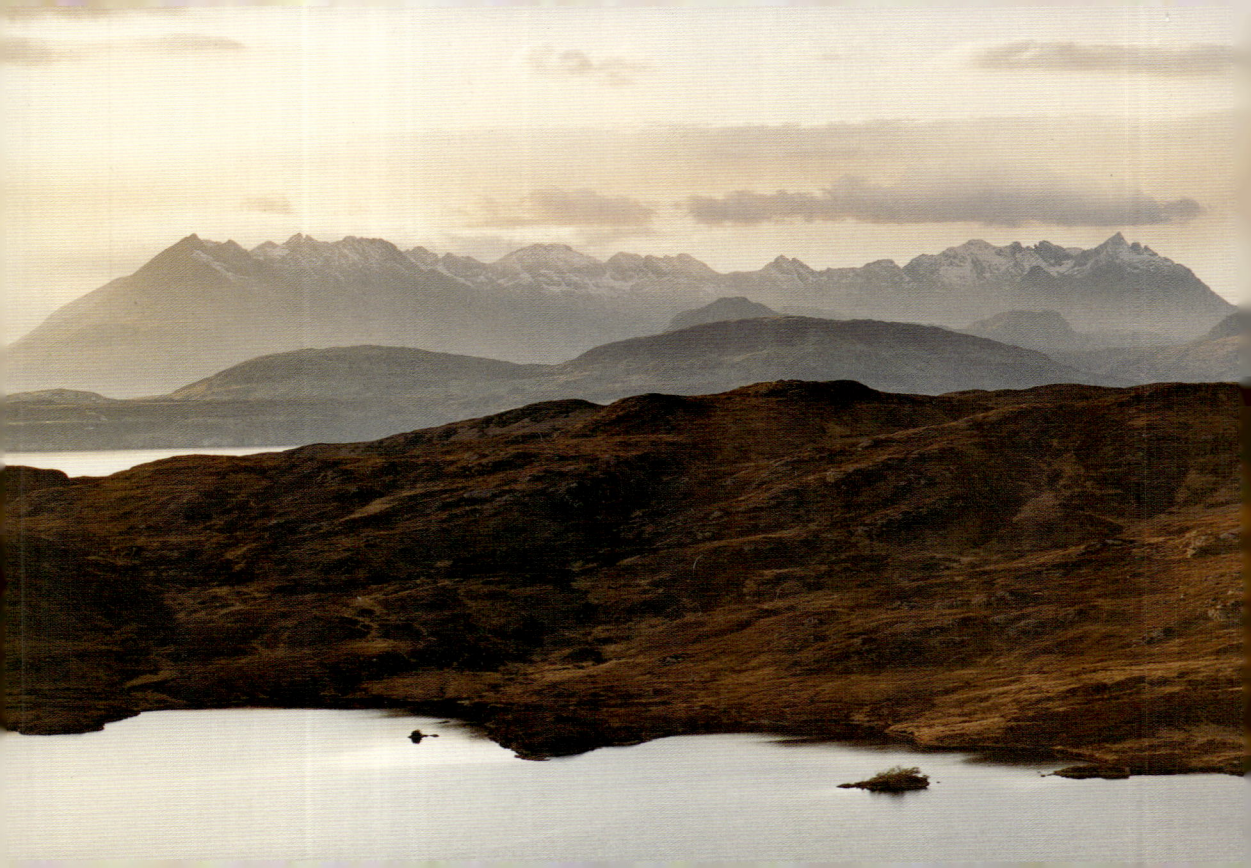

The ISLE of SKYE

The Isle of Skye is full of surprises. It is the largest of the Inner Hebrides and an island of rare beauty with a long and dramatic history.

According to legend, Skye takes its name from the Gaelic for 'The Winged Isle', but even the most detailed and romantic of descriptions cannot do justice to the breathtaking splendour that is Scotland's island jewel.

Whether crossing by bridge at Kyleakin or the more leisurely sea routes from Armadale, Glenelg and Uig, the road to Skye and the magnificent vistas that slowly unfold before you, are but a fraction of the pleasures that await.

The spectacular Cuillin Hills dominate the landscape, an imposing yet reassuring constant of island life. In the south there is the historic home of Clan Macdonald of Sleat, while in the north the ancestral stronghold of Clan Macleod and their 800-year-old fortress Dunvegan Castle. In the far north-east the extraordinary geological marvels of 'The Old Man of Storr' and the Quirang beckon.

The picturesque town of Portree is the 'capital' of Skye, and there are many other delights to discover. The stunning views from Elgol, the earthy intensity of Talisker (Skye's only malt whisky), and a natural environment of mountains, glens and lochs that provide home for an abundance of wildlife, from dolphins to golden eagles.

In 1746, Bonnie Prince Charlie, dressed as Flora Macdonald's maid, fled to Skye to evade the pursuing Redcoats, forever intertwining the island with the romance and tragedy of the Jacobites. However, the history of Skye is far deeper and richer than any one single event, and the journey to this most iconic of islands remains as evocative and magical today as it did more than 250 years ago.

So whether it is your first visit, or the most recent of many, you can be guaranteed that the Isle of Skye will surpass all your expectations, and that is perhaps the greatest surprise of all.

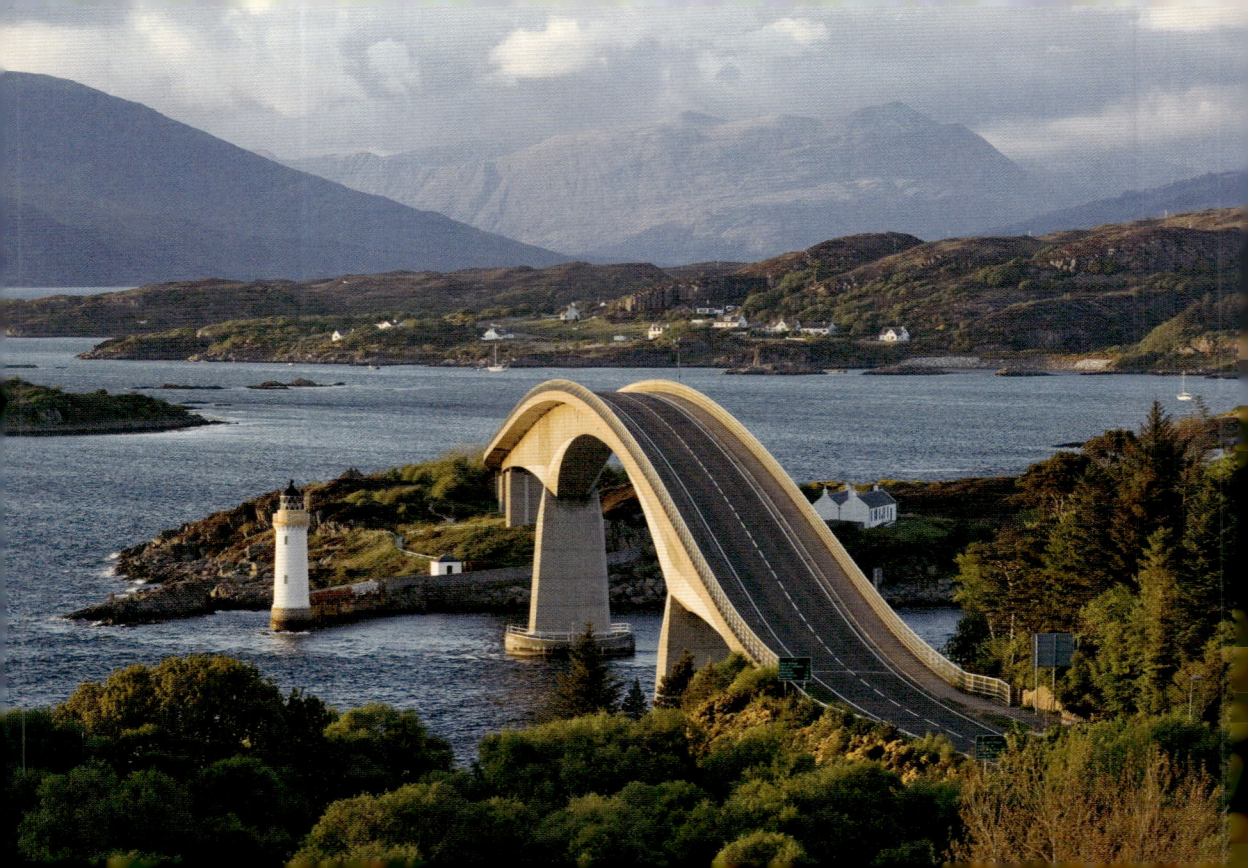

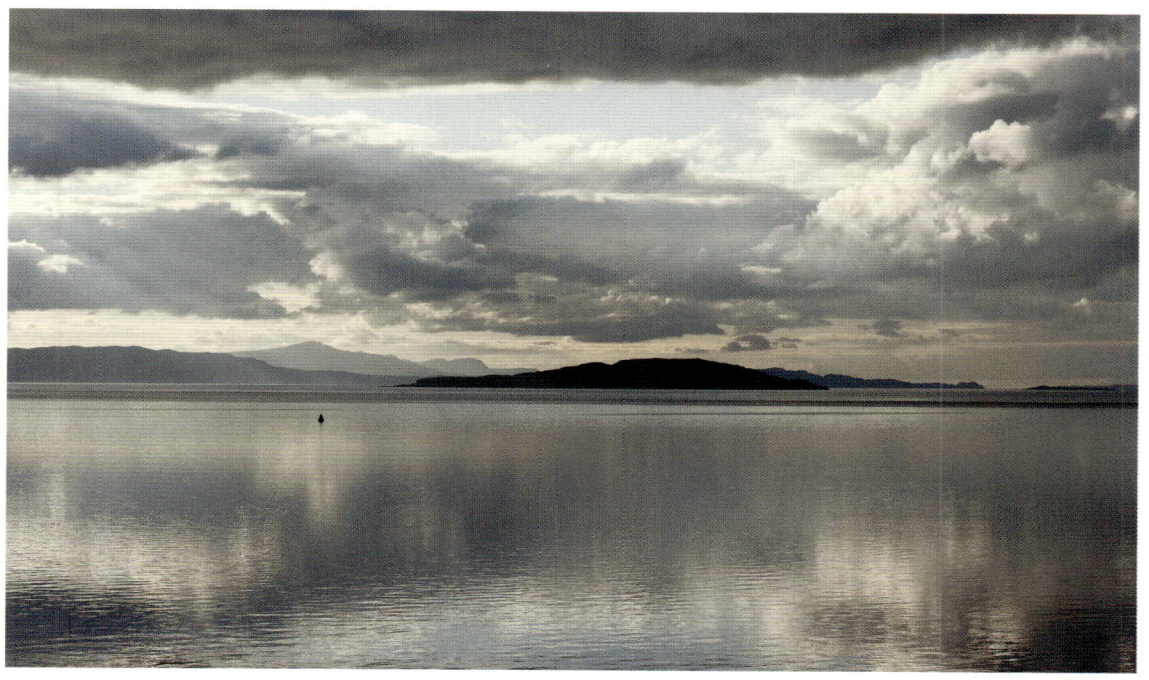

THE SKYE BRIDGE – with Wester Ross beyond (left), and looking north-west from the bridge (above).

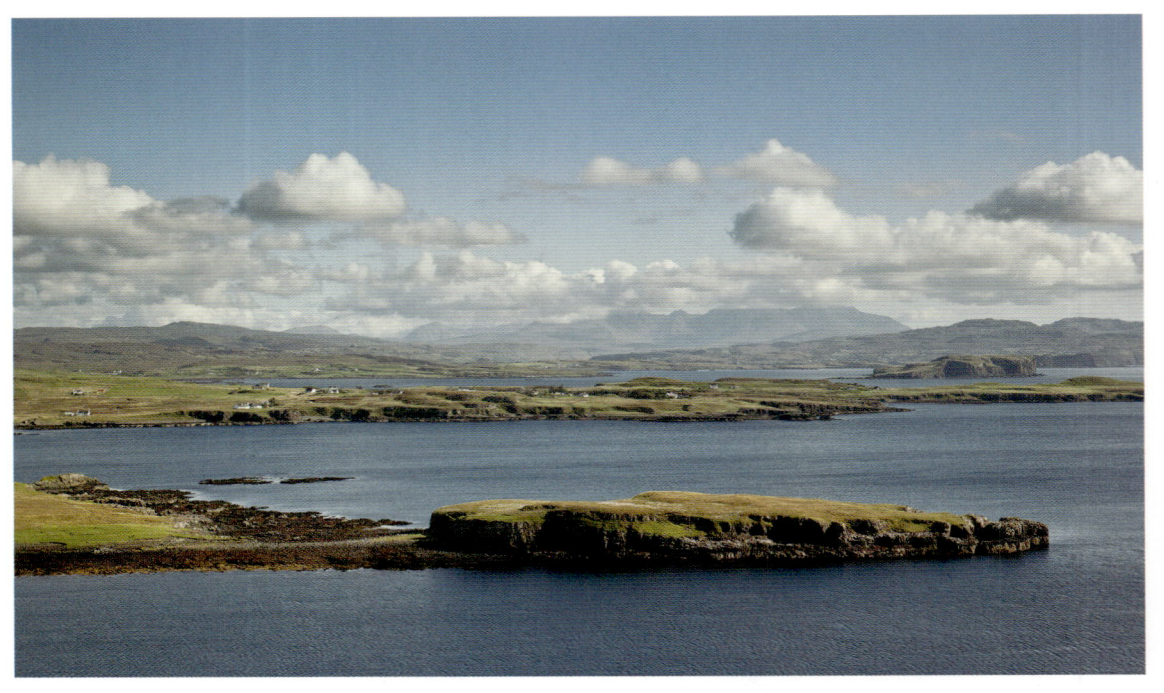

Roag Island, Harlosh and Tarner Island, LOCH BRACADALE – with the Cuillin Hills in the distance.

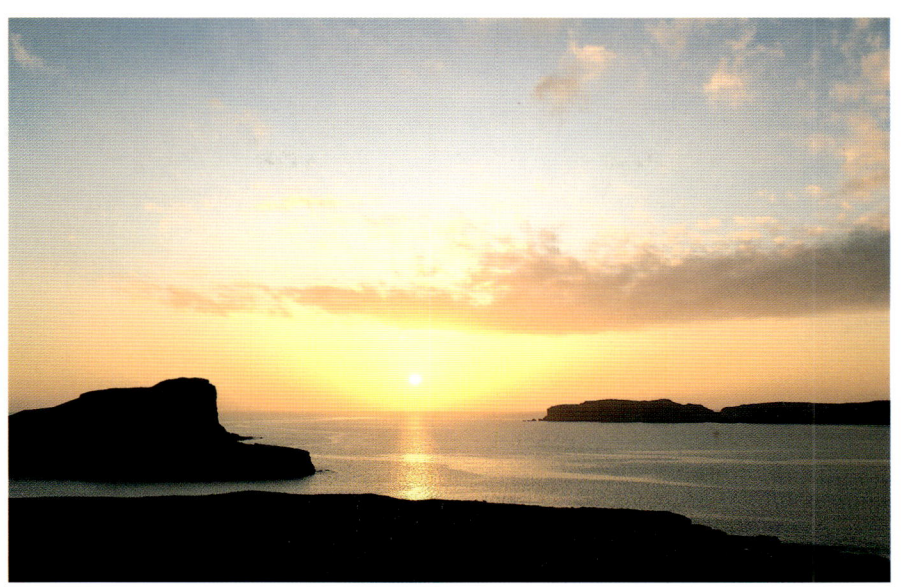

Oronsay and Wiay, LOCH BRACADALE – There are several uninhabited islands in the shallow waters of Loch Bracadale, a sea loch on the west coast of Skye, including Oronsay (accessible by foot at low tide) and Wiay, both silhouetted here at sunset.

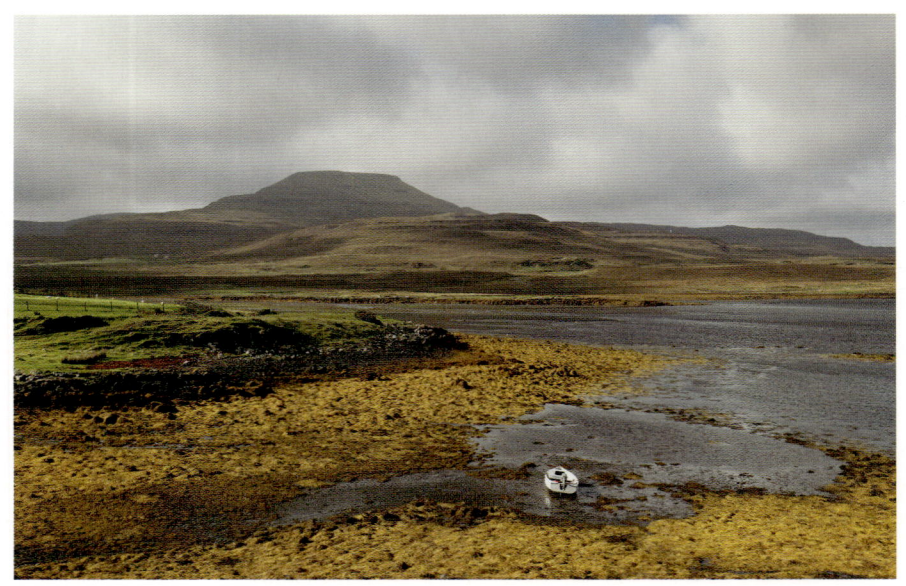

DUNVEGAN CASTLE (right) – the seat and ancestral home of the Clan Macleod. Their name was given to the Macleod's Tables, two recognisable hills to the south-west, about which there are many local legends. Above is HEALABHAL MHÒR (Macleod's Table North) beyond Loch Dunvegan.

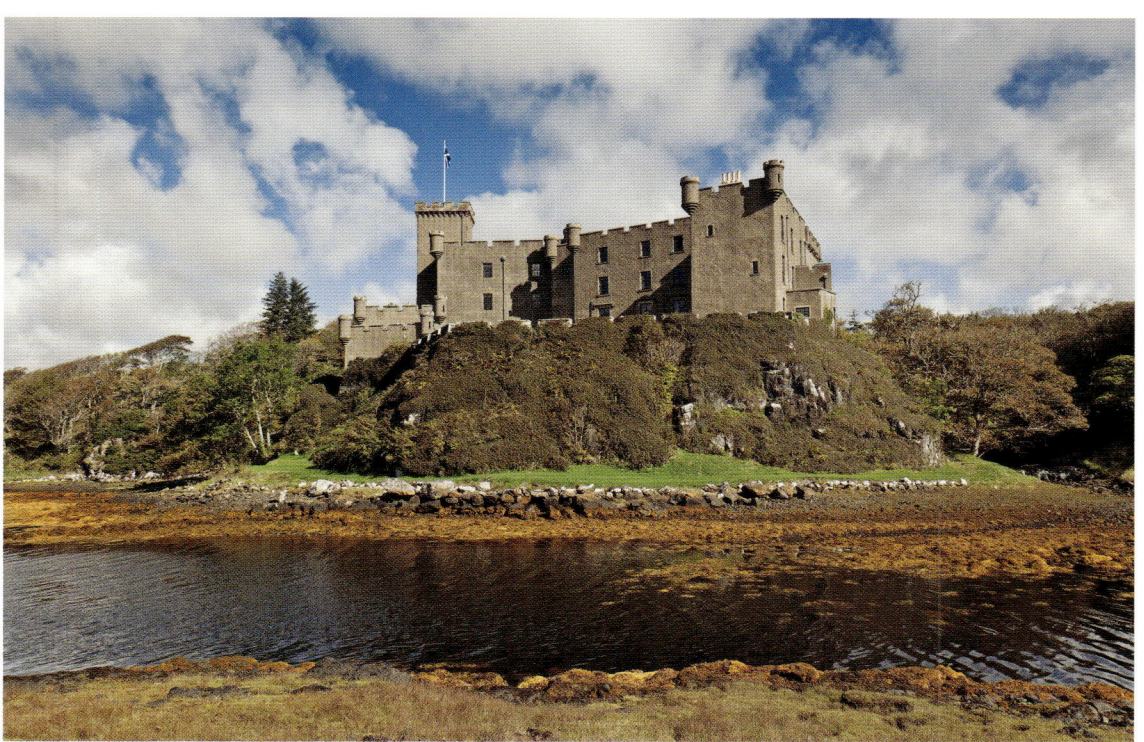

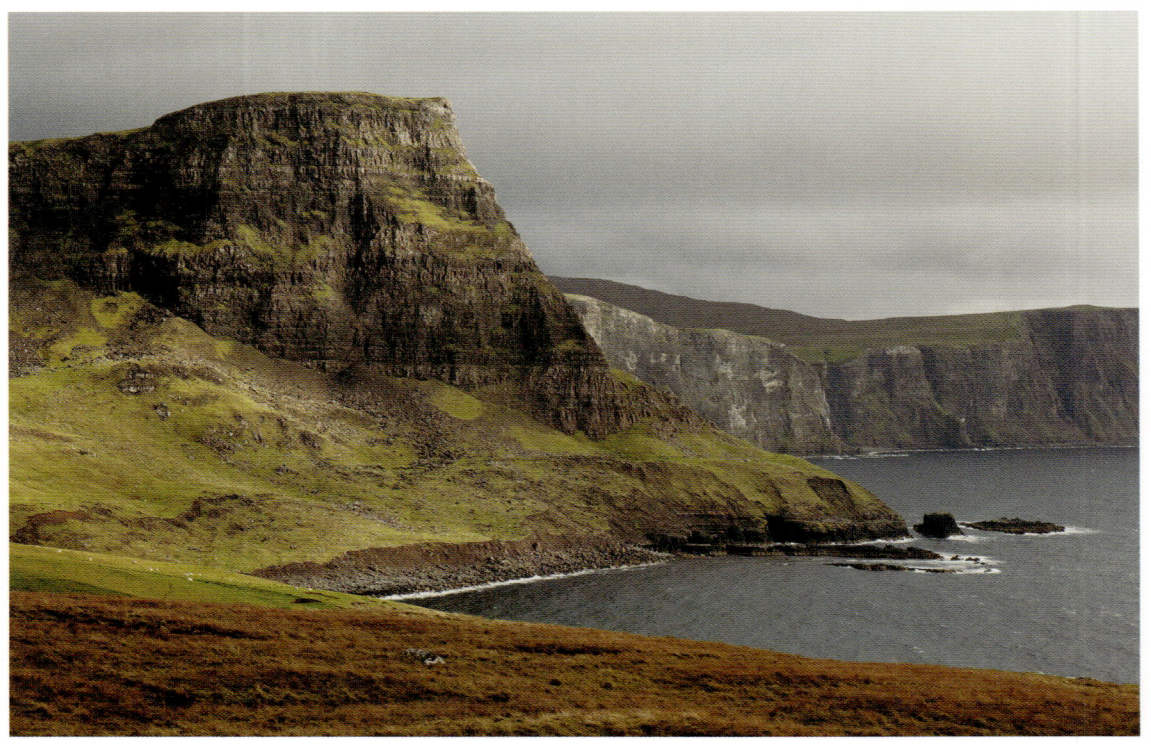

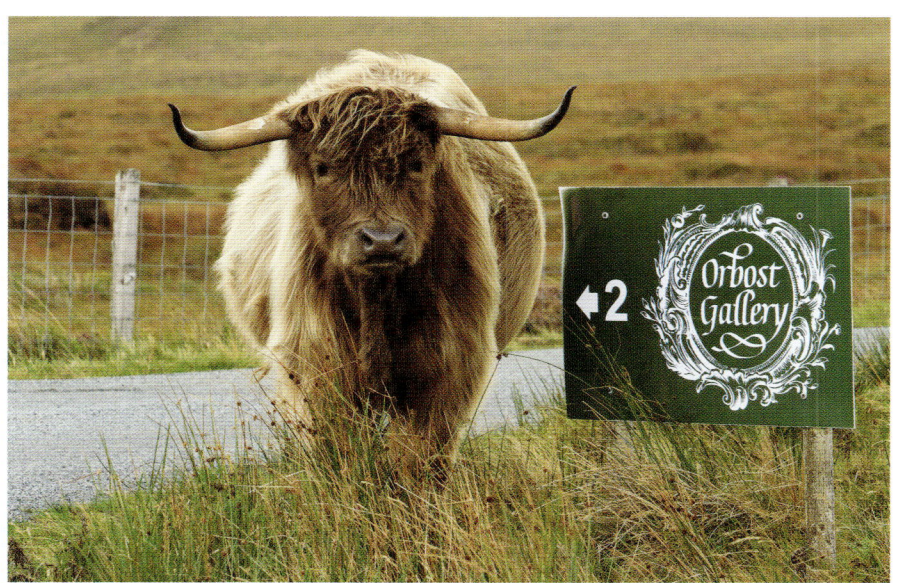

DUIRINISH, or Diùranais in Scottish Gaelic, meaning "deer headland", is the island's westernmost peninsula with the imposing Waterstein Head (left) standing resolutely against all of Skye's elements. A sedate HIGHLAND COW (above) – a Skye resident.

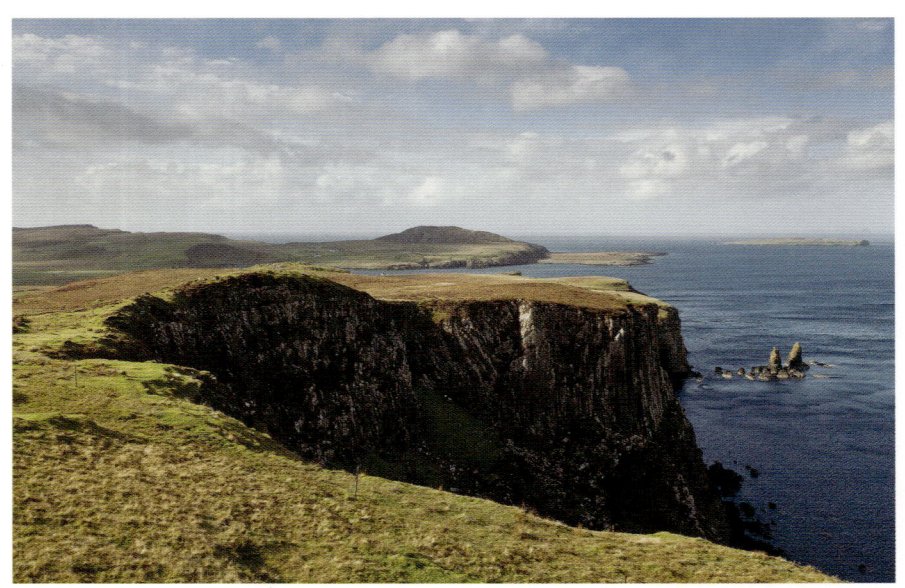

TROTTERNISH – looking towards 'The Aird' in the far north (above). Skye's northernmost peninsula lays claim to the geological marvel that is the Trotternish Ridge, an amazing landscape created by a 20-mile long landslip, as seen in the view southwards from the Quirang (right).

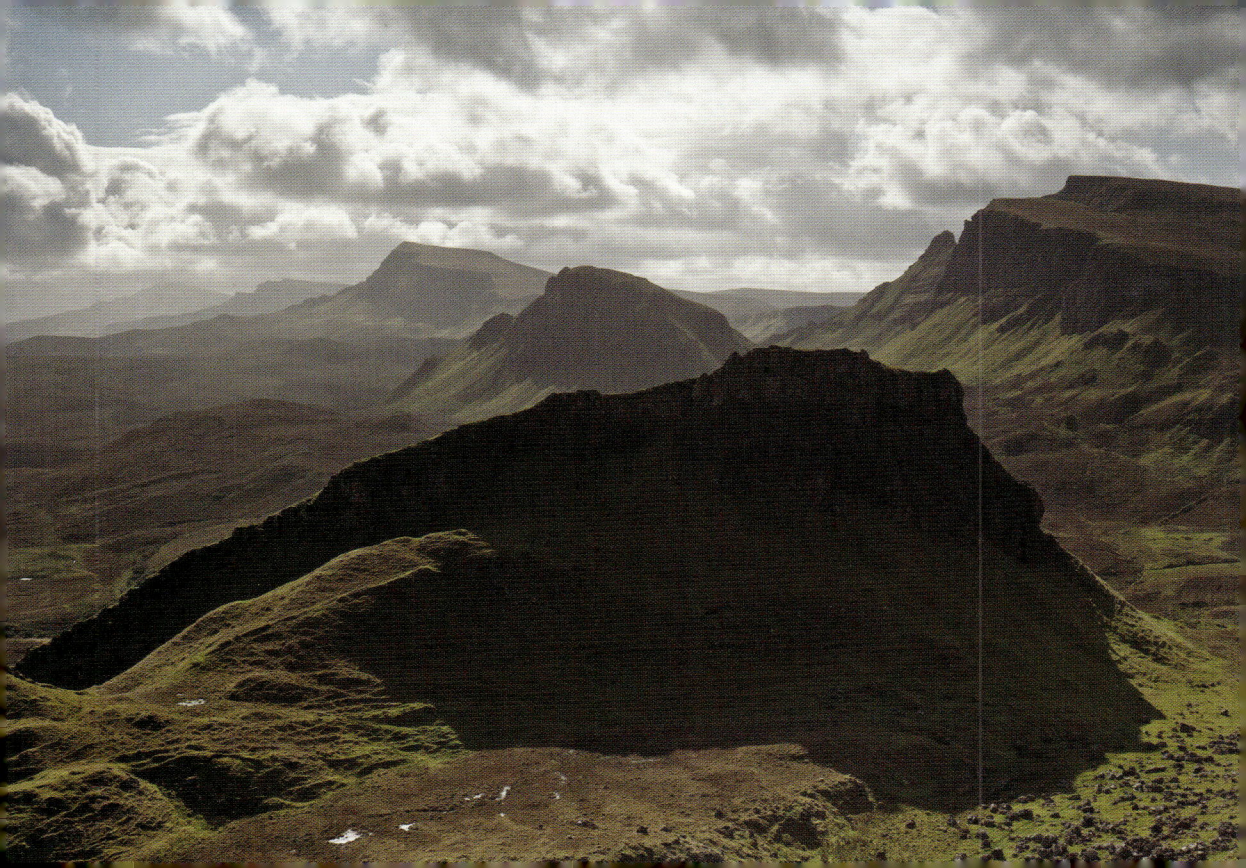

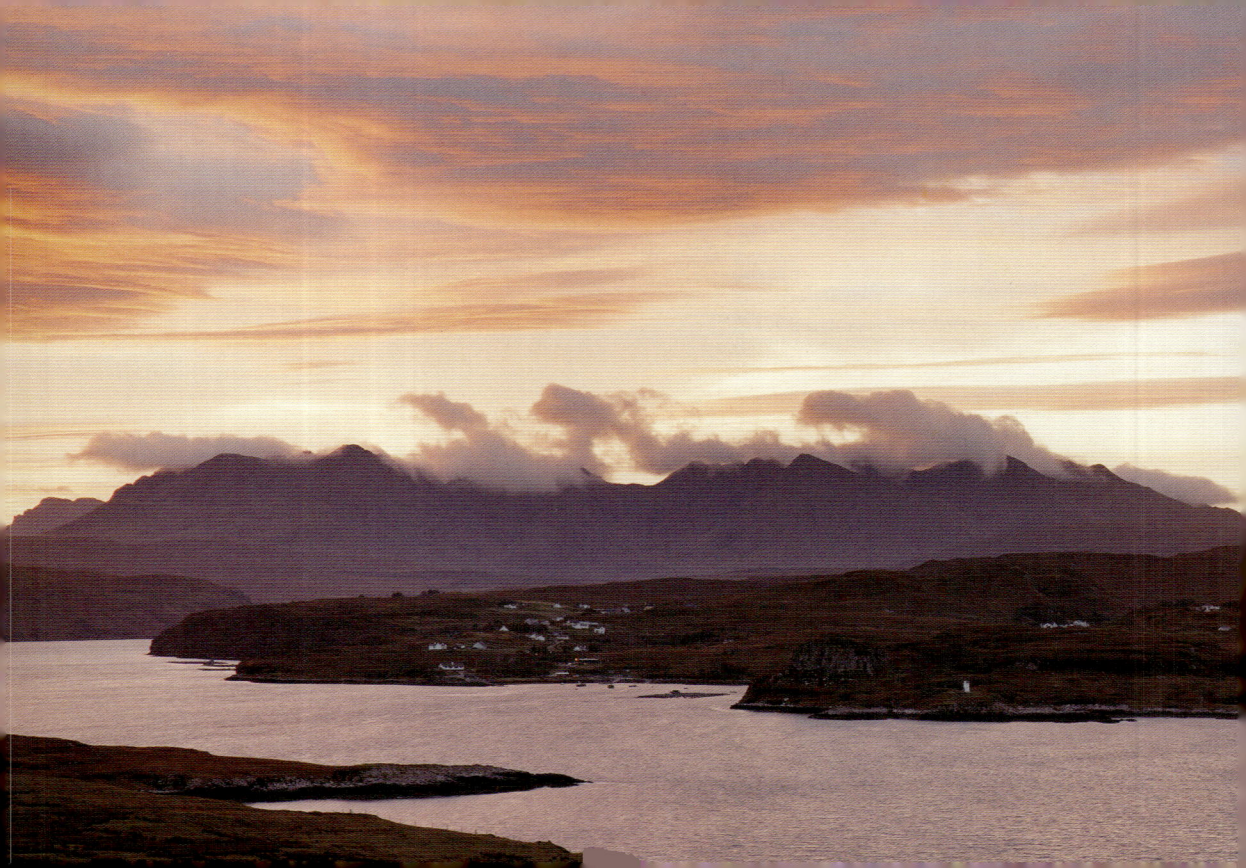

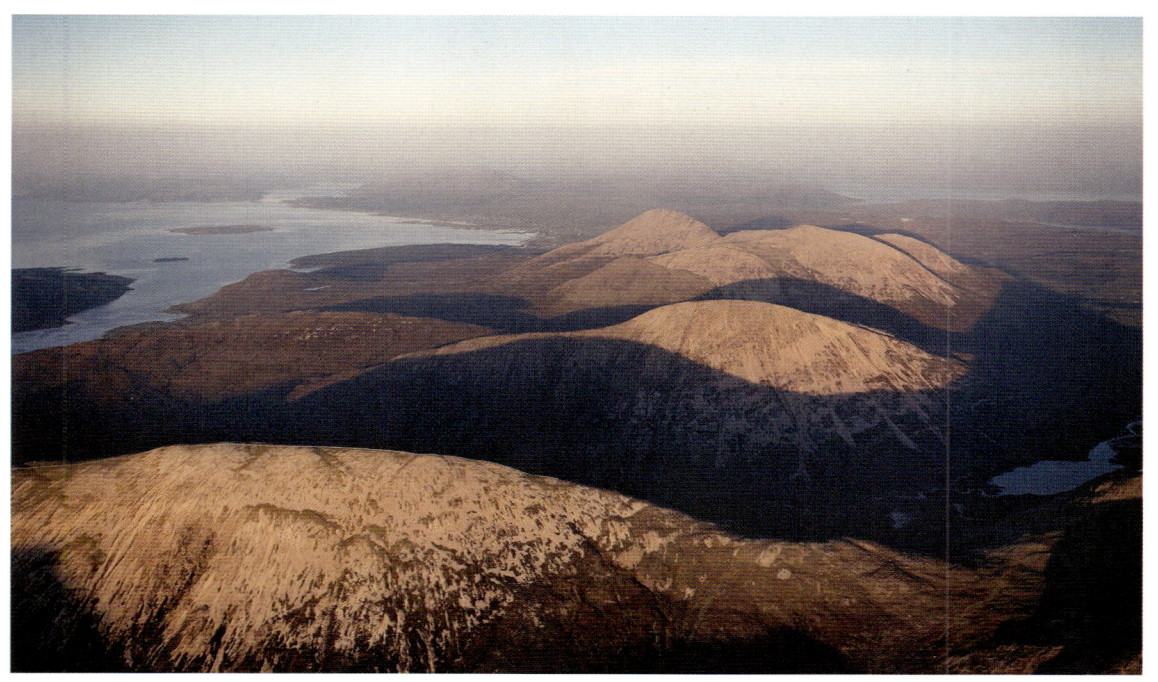

THE CUILLIN HILLS, 'The Black Cuillin', beyond Loch Harport (left), and 'THE RED CUILLIN' (above).

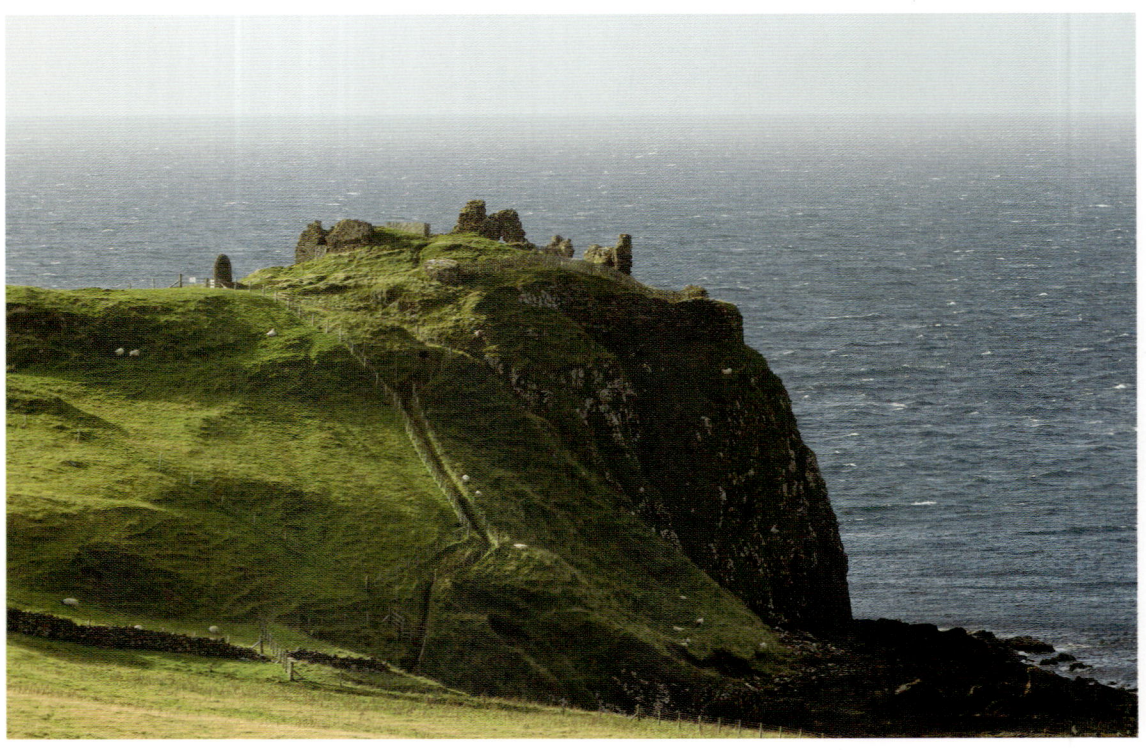

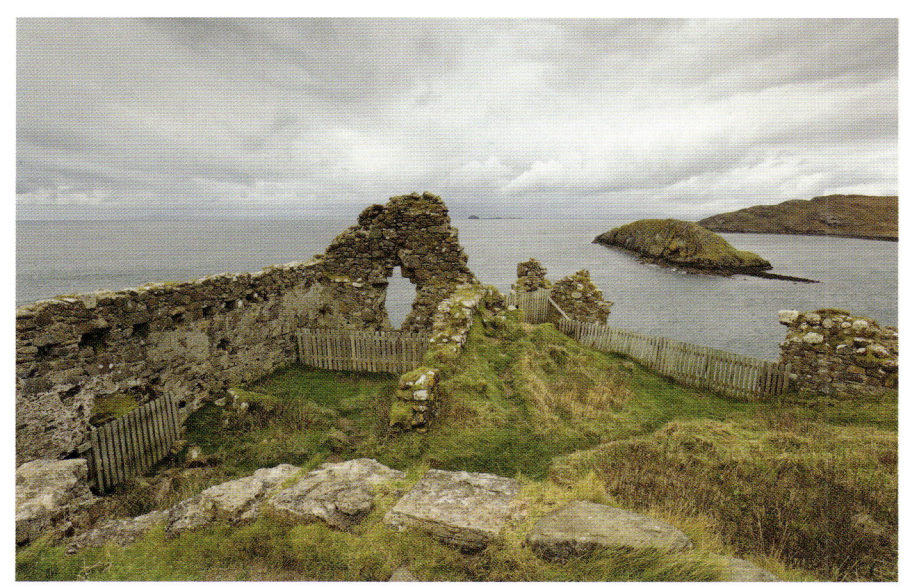

DUNTULM CASTLE, Trotternish – Built in the 14th and 15th centuries, this ruined former fortress of Clan Macdonald was finally abandoned in 1730. Travelling to Duntulm will reward the determined visitor with some of the most impressive coastal scenery on Skye.

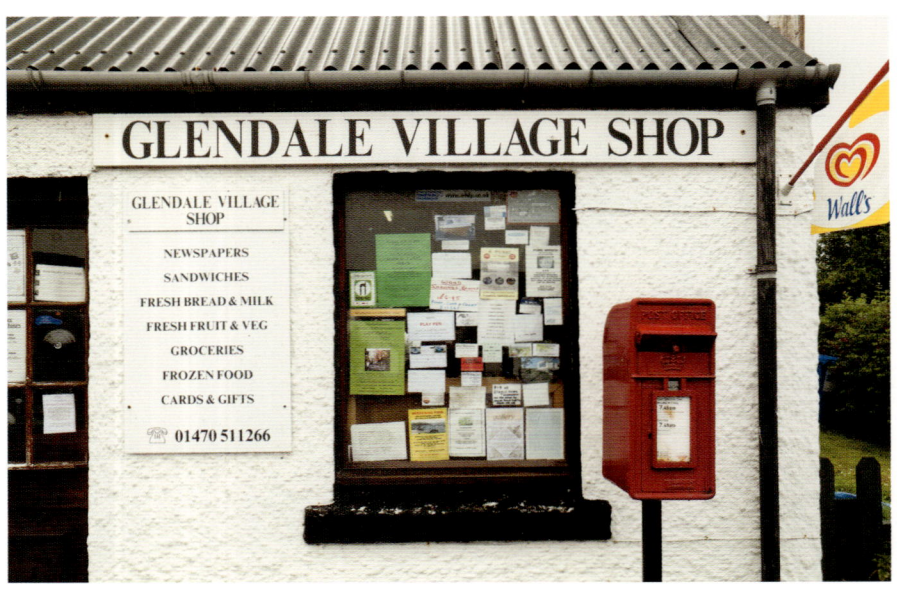

GLENDALE, Durinish – Belying its tranquil appearance, the settlement of Glendale was the location of a fierce battle between Macdonald and Macleod around 1513. In 1883 it saw local crofters take direct action against their landlords in the long campaign for land reform and crofters' rights.

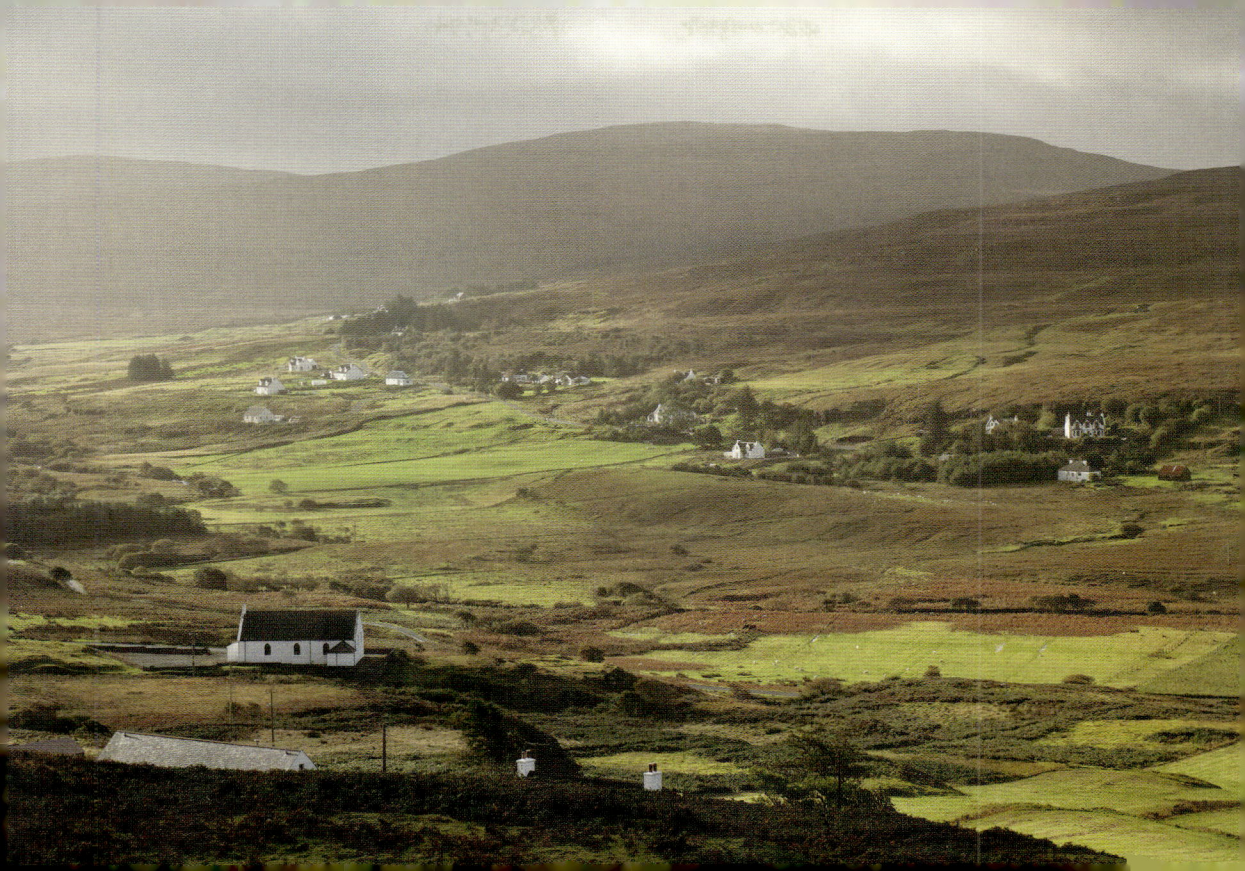

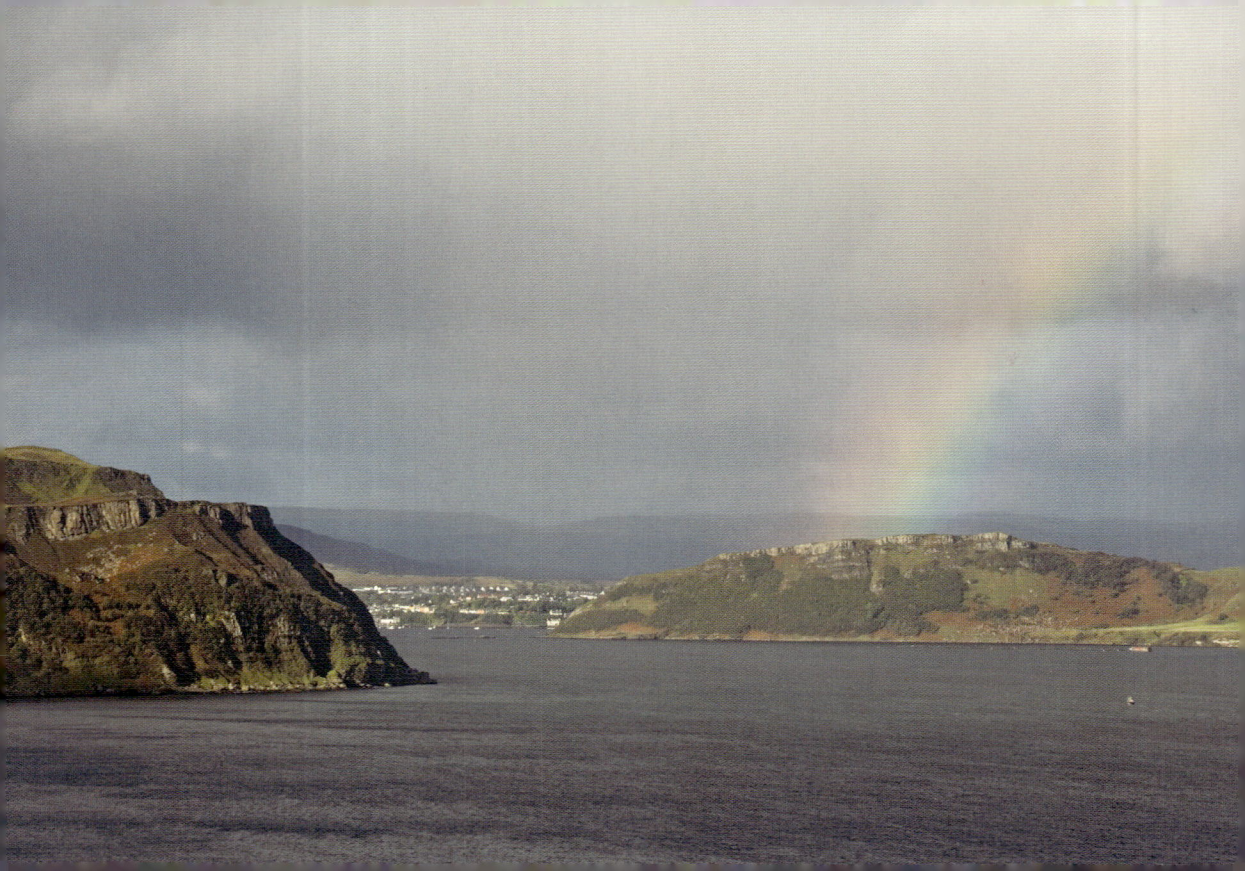

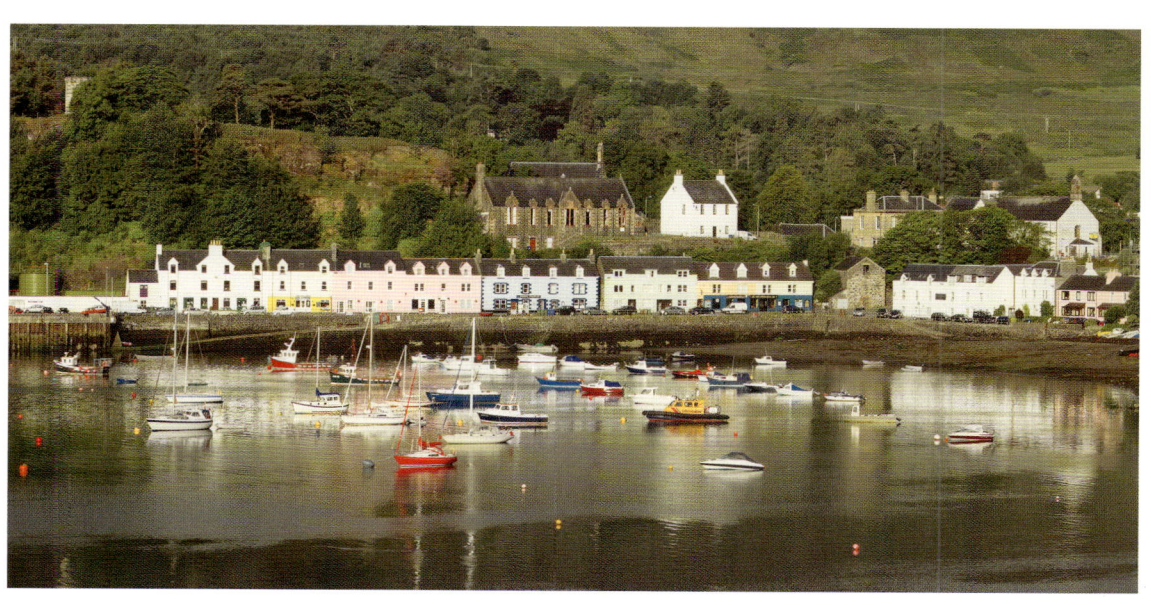

PORTREE – Nestling on the eastern coastline, the natural harbour of Portree has seen Skye's capital and principal port become the hub and heart of island life, and a historic haven for travellers and visitors from both land and sea.

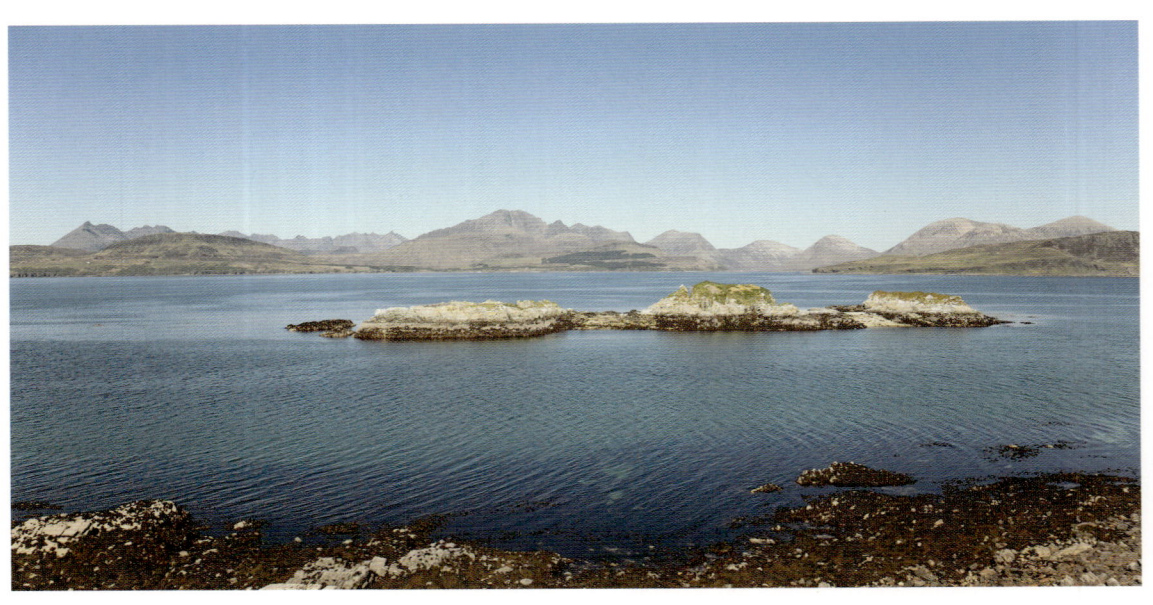

DUNSCIATH CASTLE, Sleat (right) – a Clan Macdonald castle that was abandoned in the 17th century. It has a commanding view to the north-west (above), towards the Cuillin Hills, Blà Bheinn, Ben na Caillich, and the land of Clan Macleod.

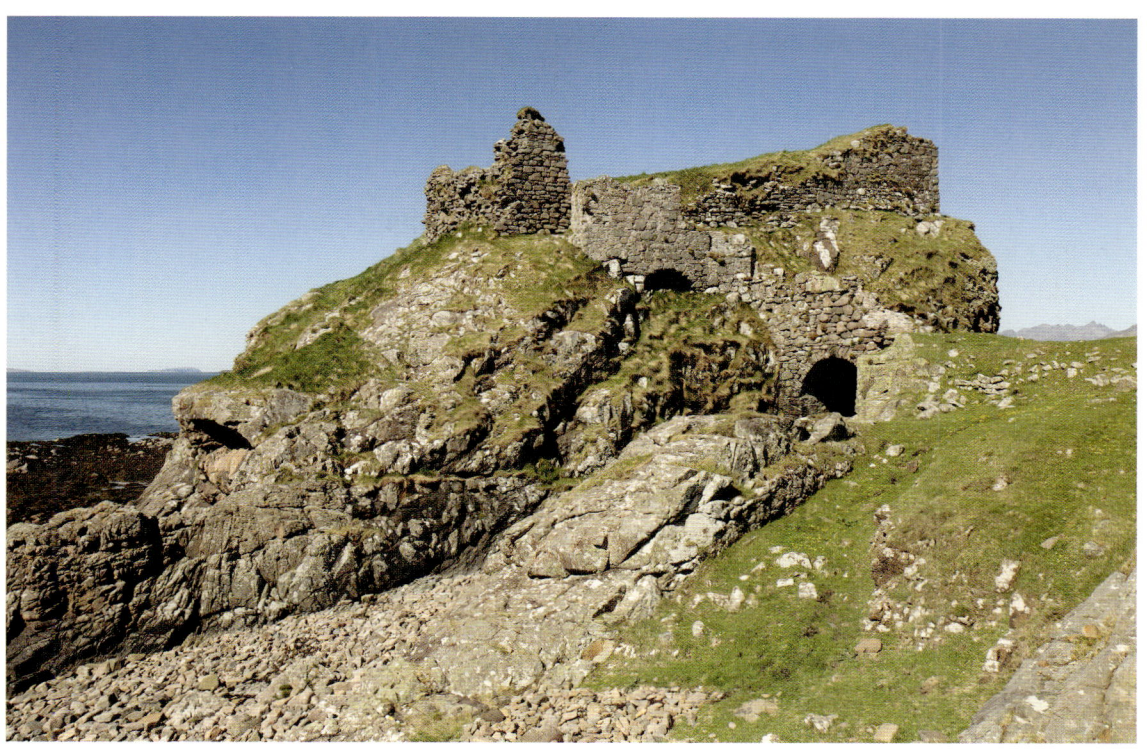

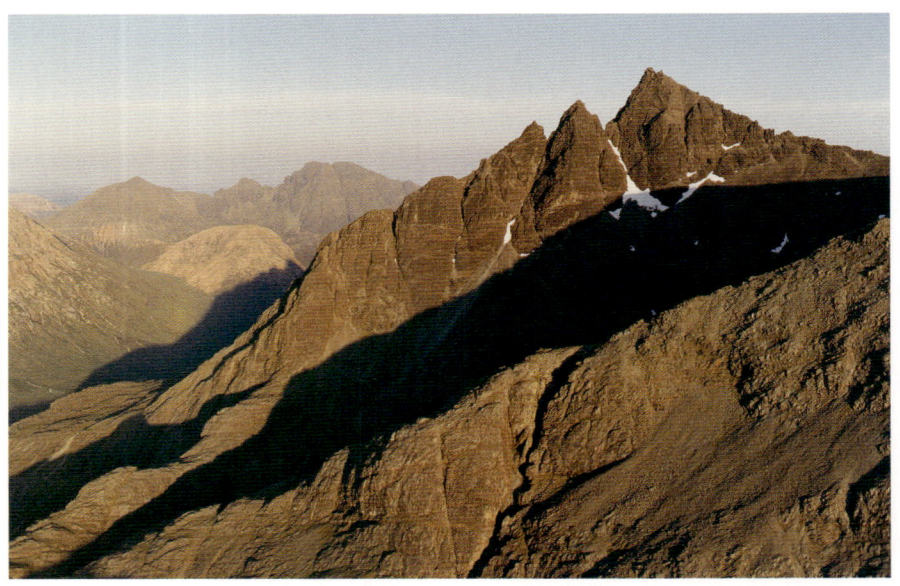

THE CUILLIN HILLS – Sgurr nan Gillean and its dramatic Pinnacle Ridge (above), and the the Cuillin Ridge from the air (right), with Loch Coruisk and Loch Scavaig beyond. With 11 Munros (mountains over 3000ft) the Cuillins are a real challange for hill walkers.

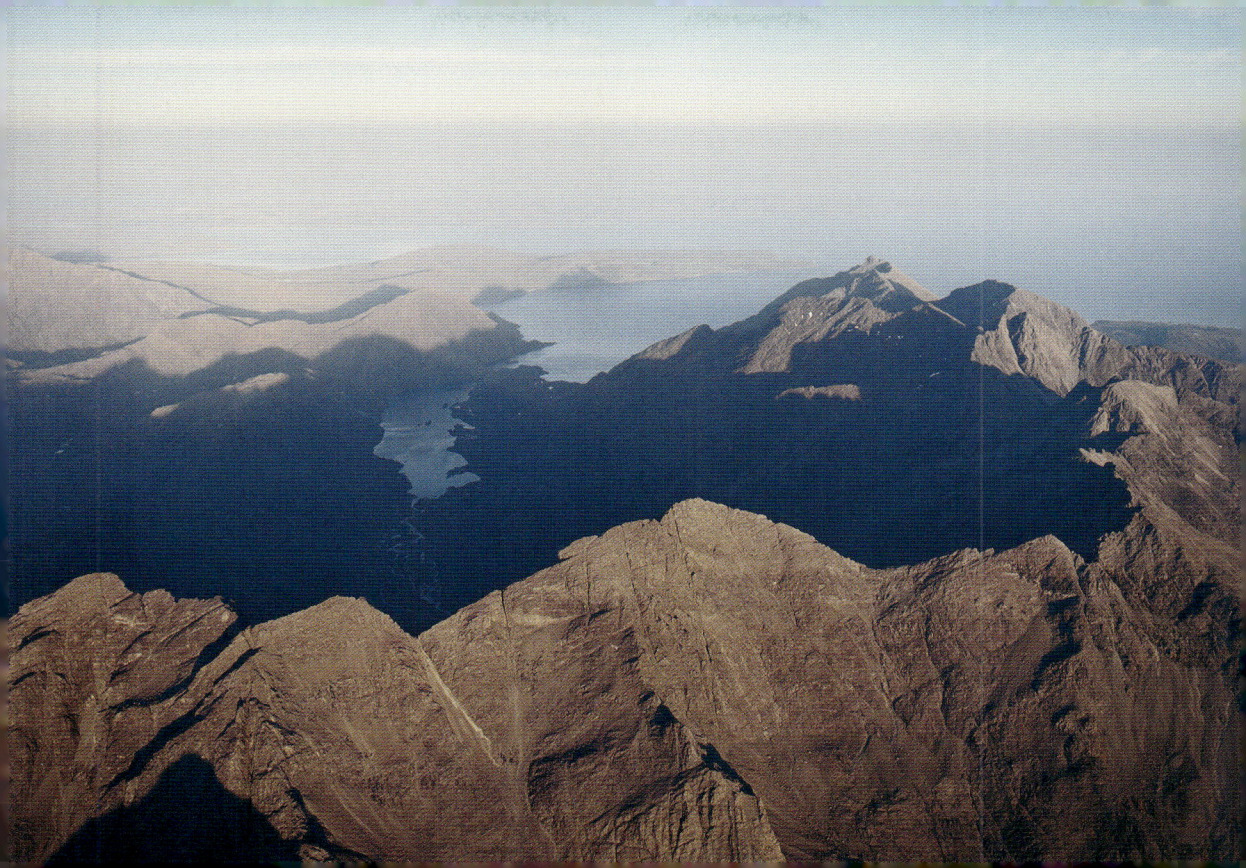

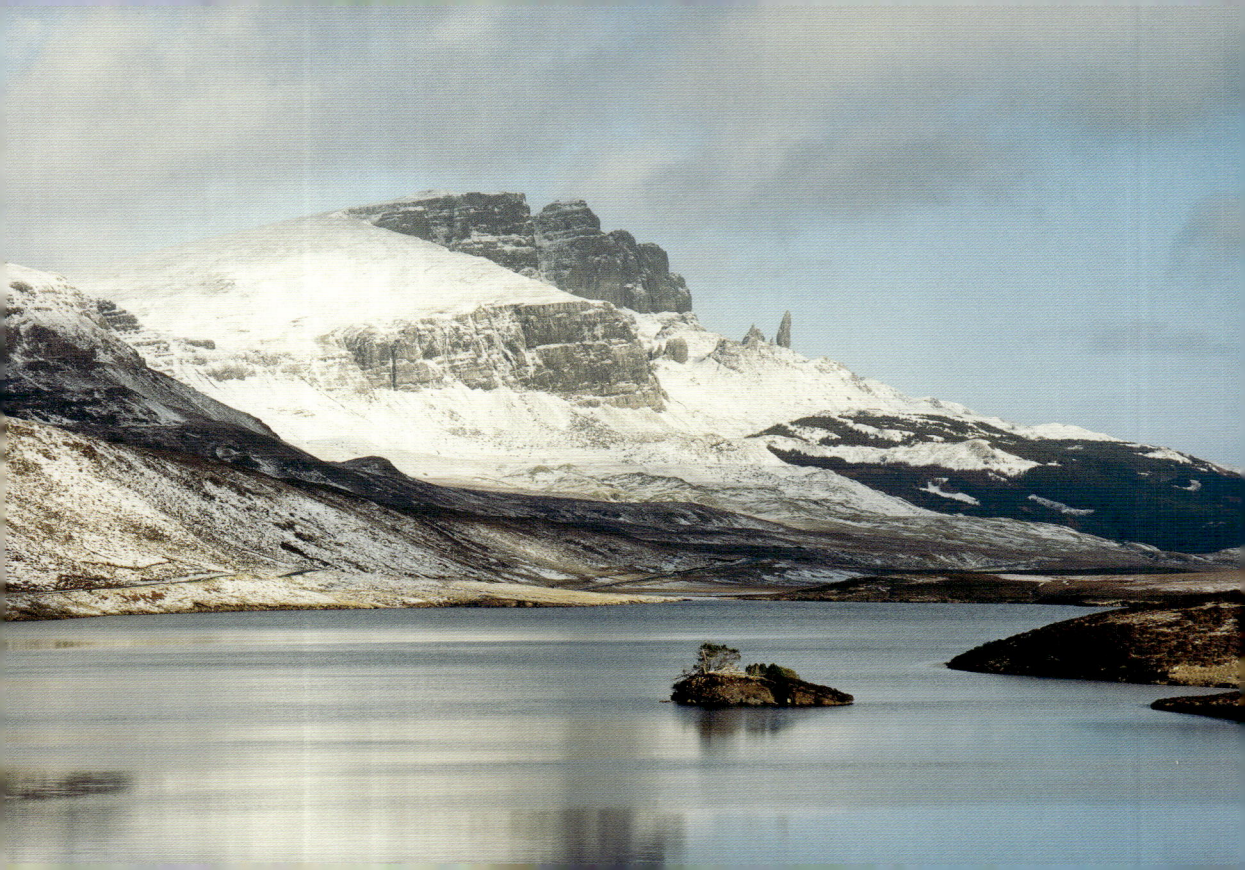

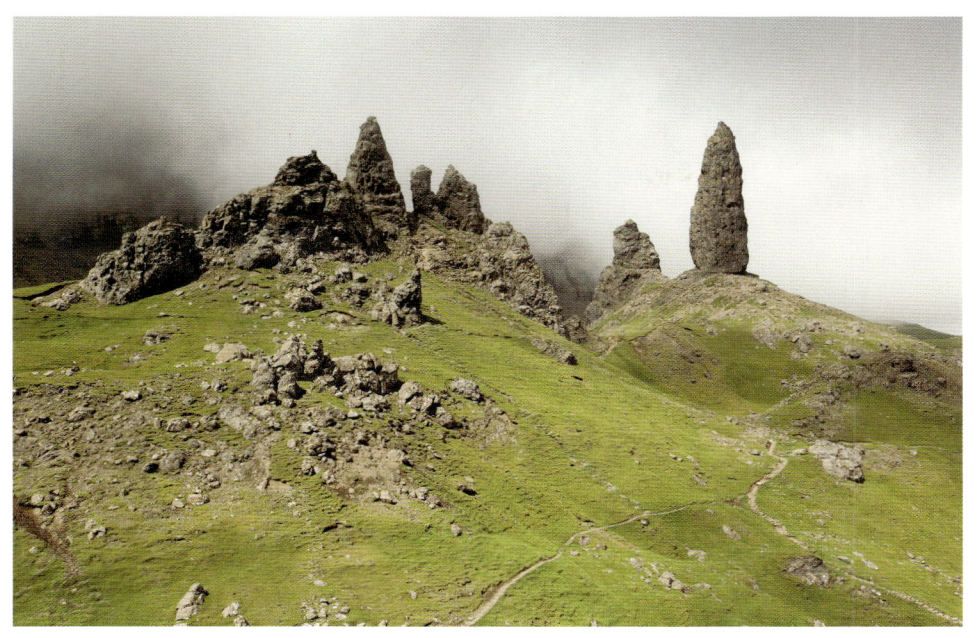

The extraordinary 'Old Man of Storr' and rock pinnacles of the Trotternish Ridge (above).
THE STORR and 'OLD MAN OF STORR', across Loch Fada, Trotternish (left).

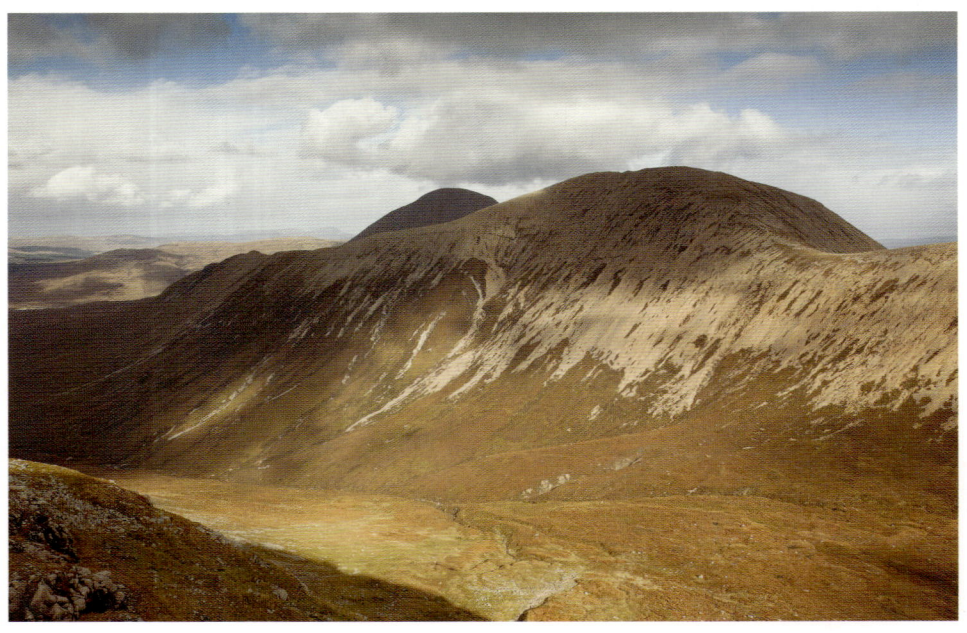

BEINN DEAG MHEADHONACH and GLAMAIG, from Marsco, Red Cuillin (above).
The imposing peak of MARSCO towering above Glen Sligachan (right).

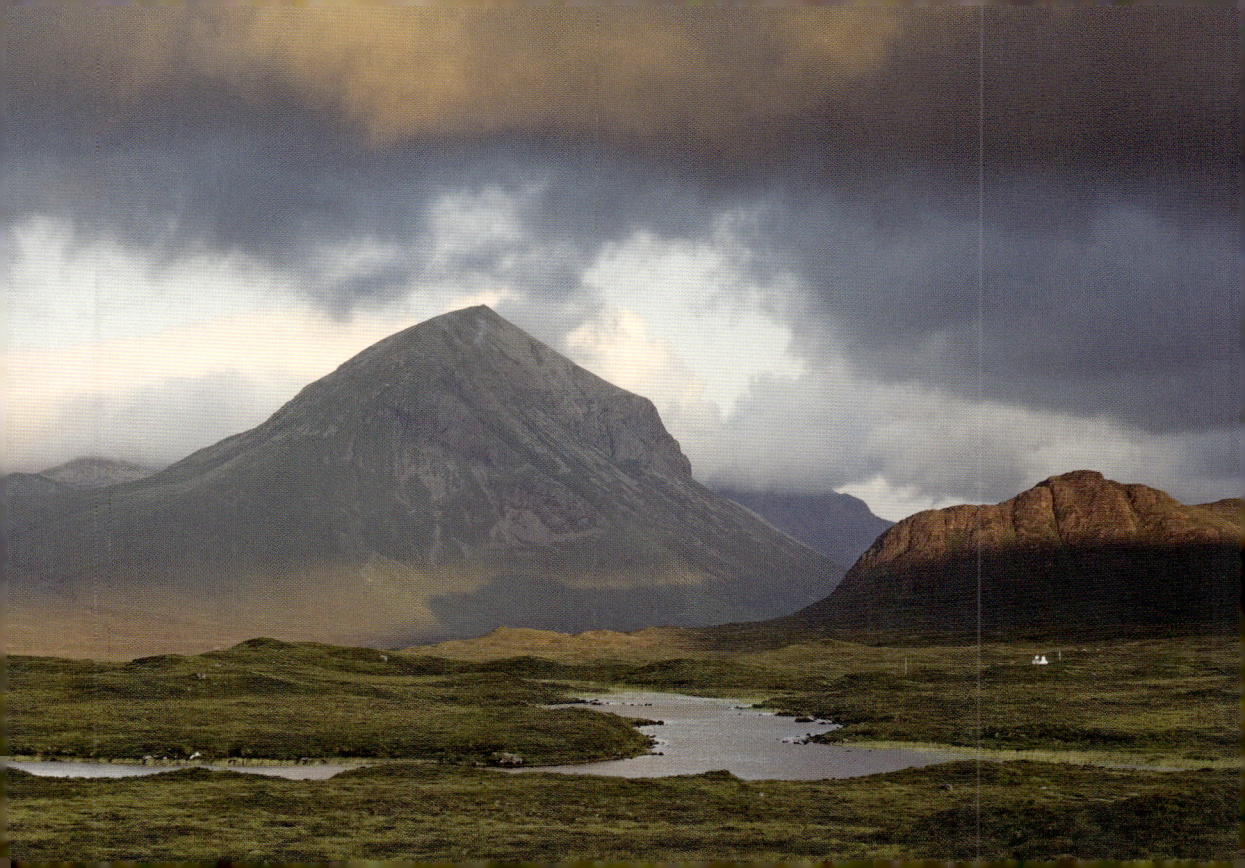

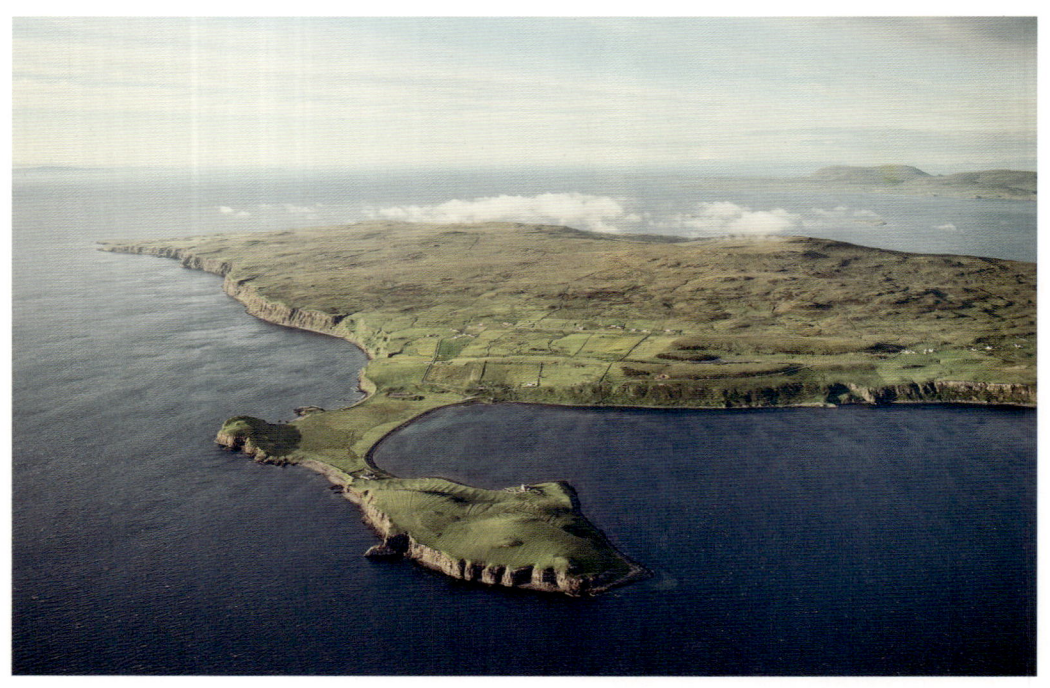

Ardmore Point, WATERNISH (above), and Ben Dearg, TROTTERNISH (right).

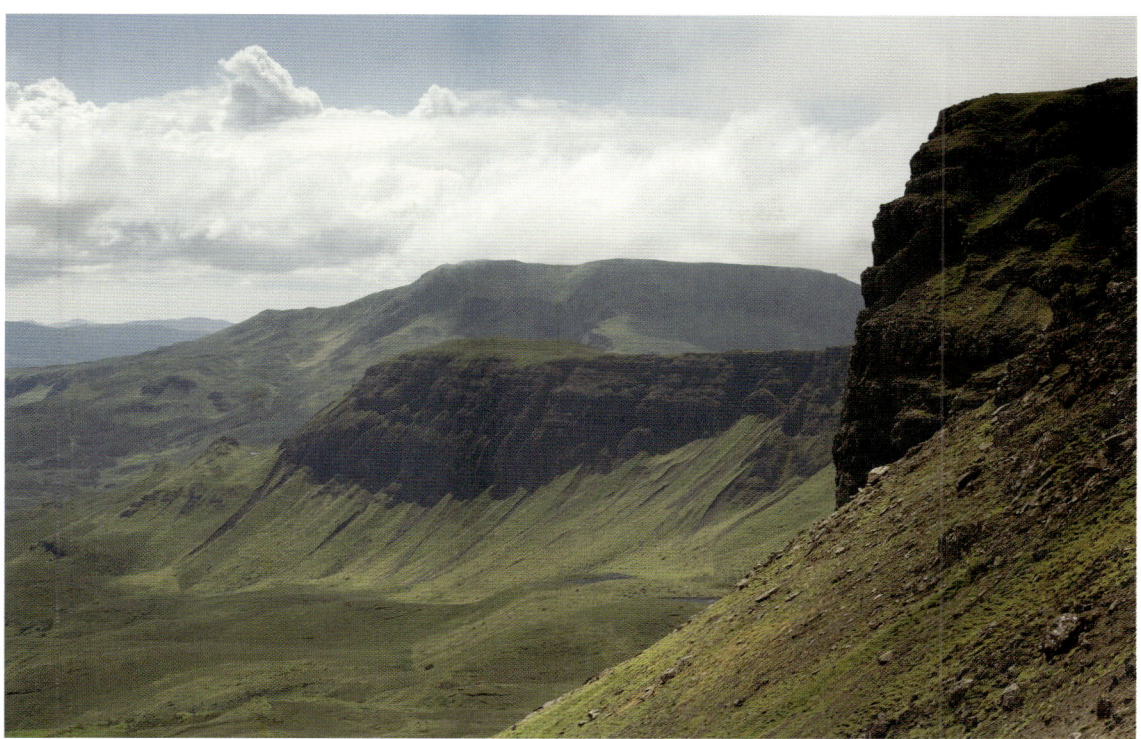

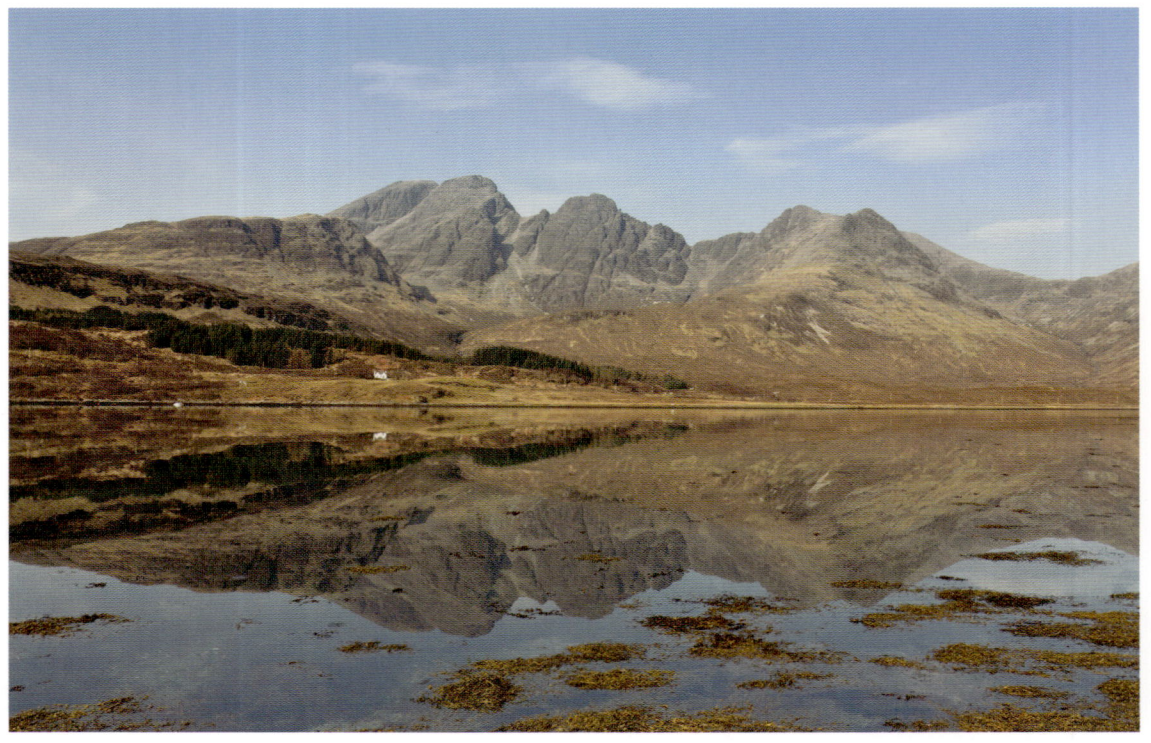

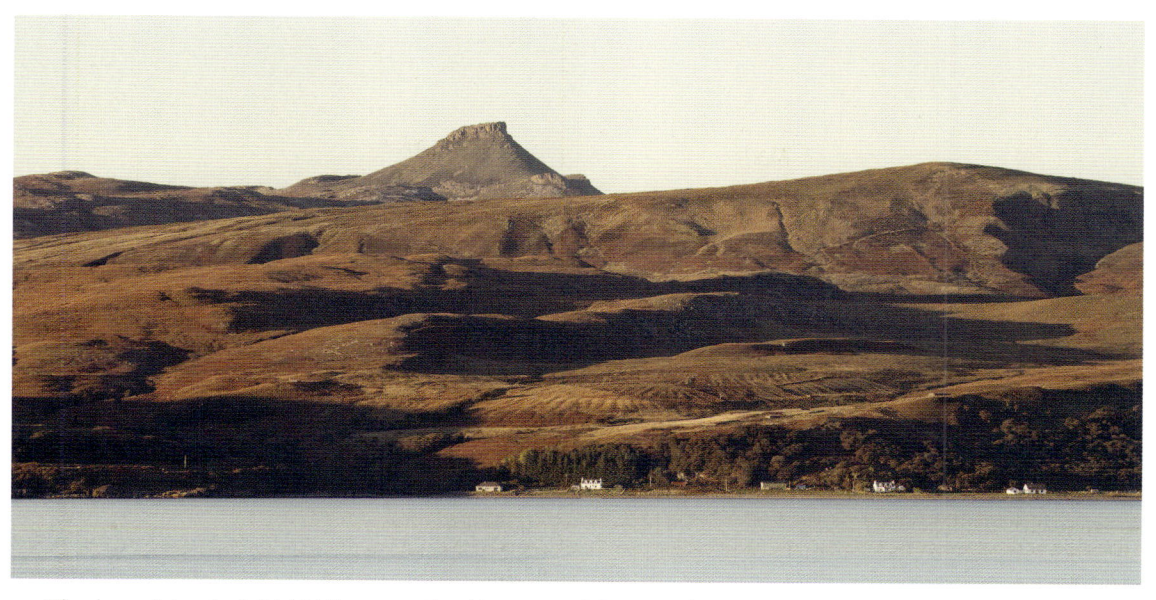

The long island of RAASAY across the Narrows of Raasay, from Sconser where the ferry departs.

BLÀ BHEINN across Loch Slapin stands in splendid isolation to the east of the Cuillin Hills (left).

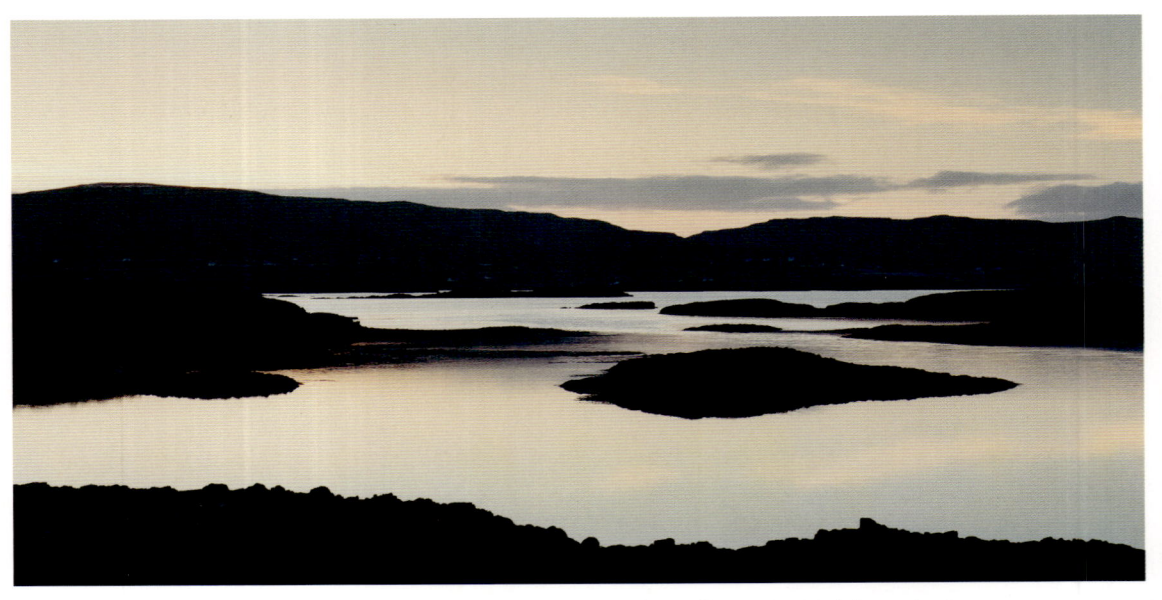

Looking across LOCH DUNVEGAN towards Colbost, Duirinish at dusk.

THE CUILLIN HILLS from the north above Sligachan (right).

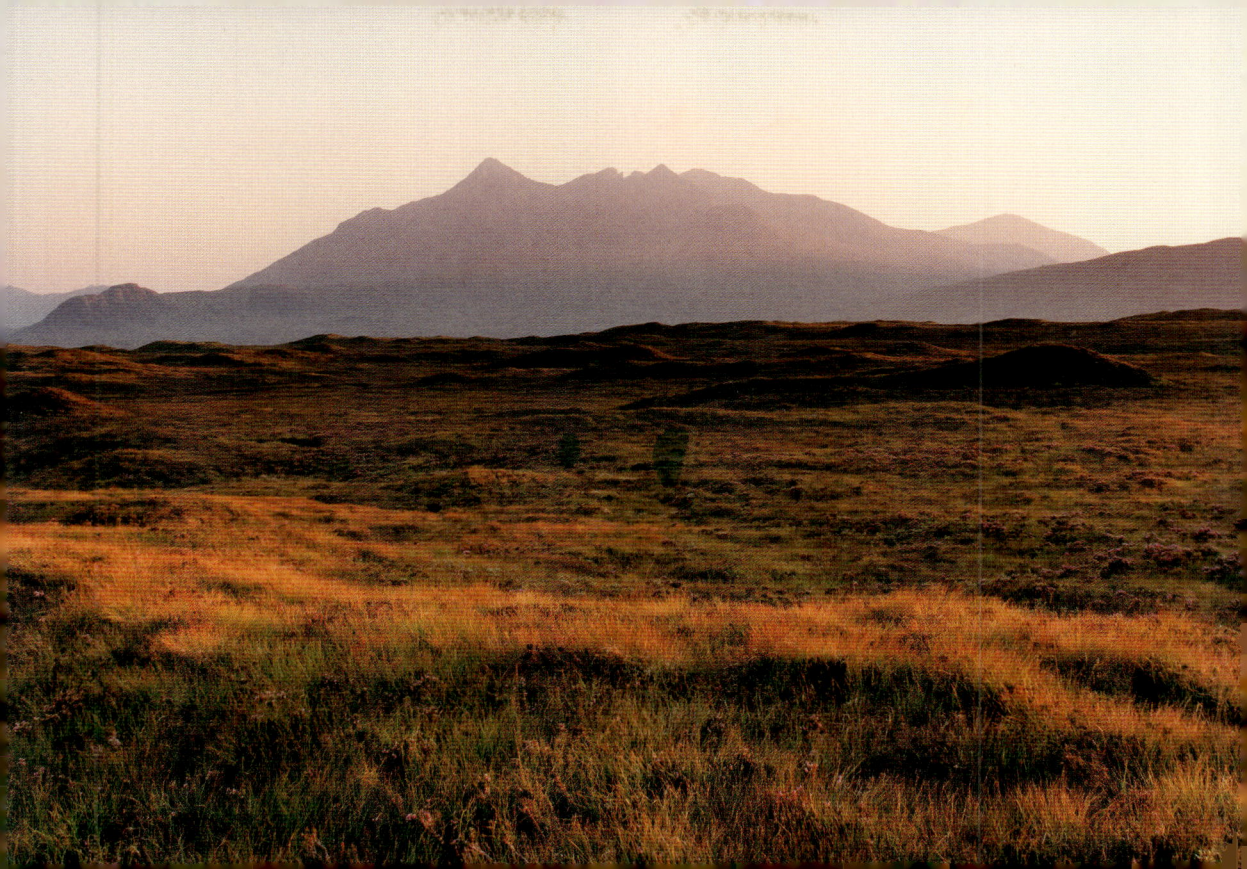

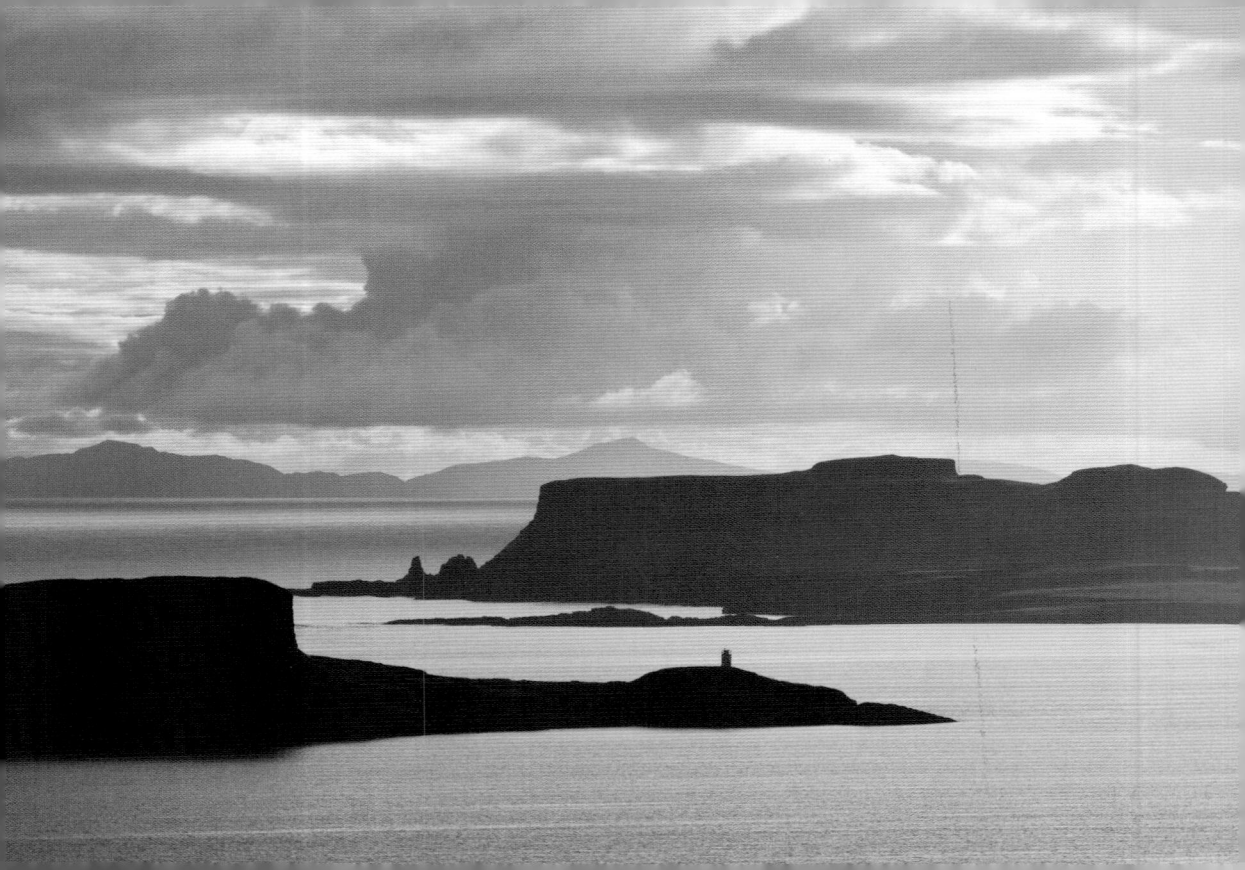

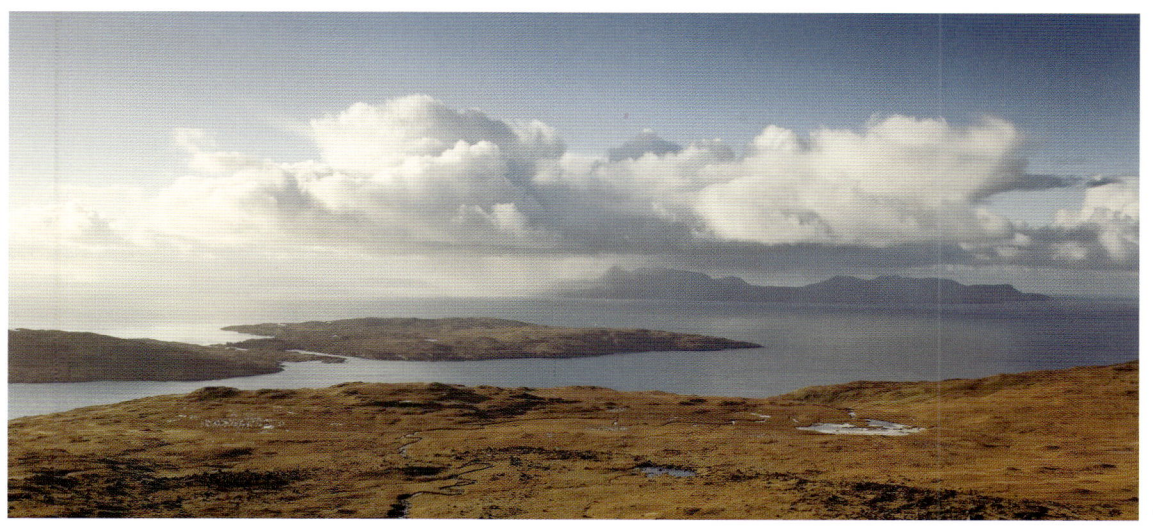

The islands of SOAY, EIGG and RÙM from the southern slopes of the Cuillin Hills.

ARDTRECK POINT and ORONSAY, Loch Bracadale (left) – with the Western Isles in the distance.

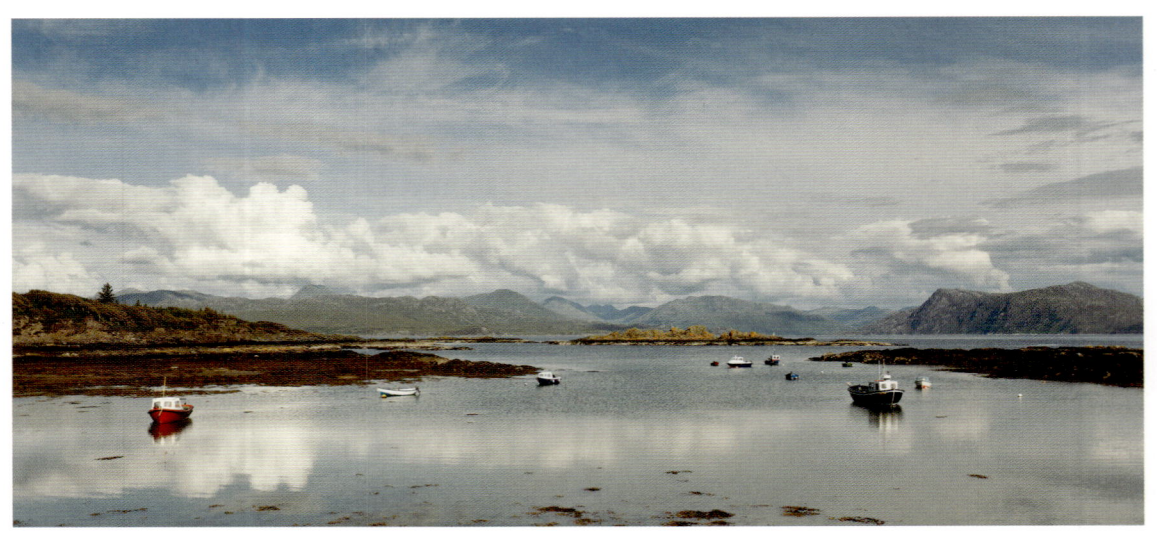

ARMADALE BAY, Sleat (above) – On the Skye side of the Sound of Sleat (right), Armadale is the disembarkation point for arrivals by ferry from Mallaig on the mainland. Since the building of the Skye Bridge, this is now one of the more romantic ways to 'go over the sea to Skye'.

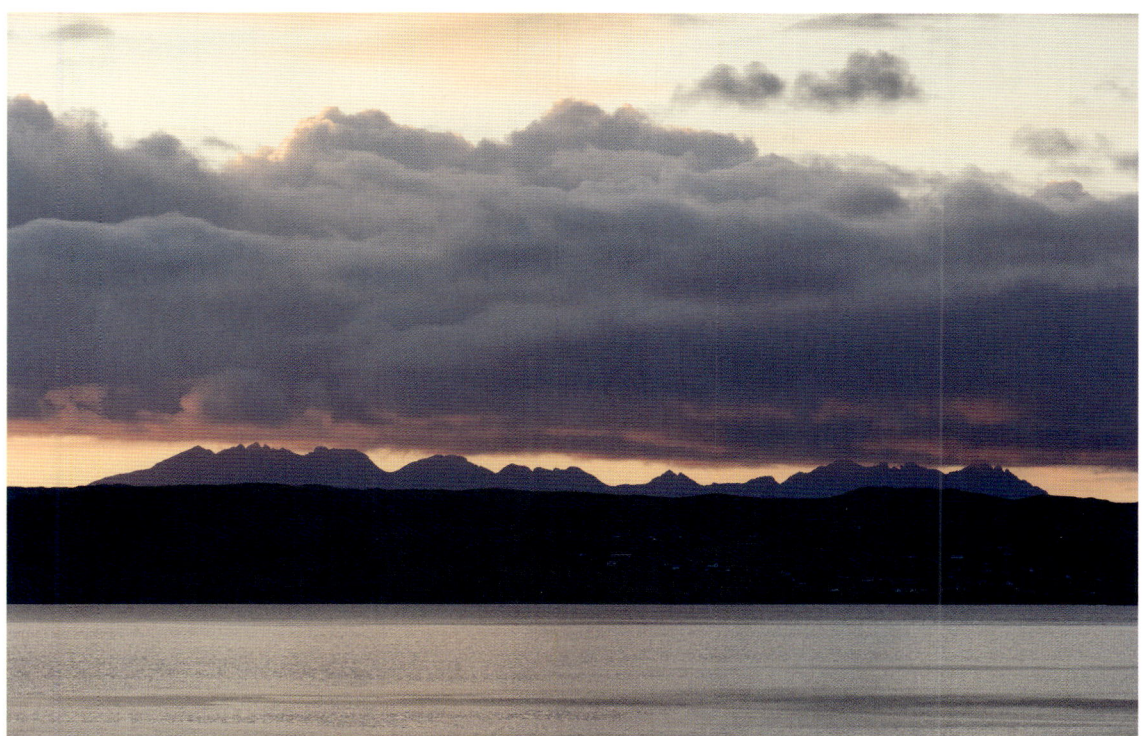

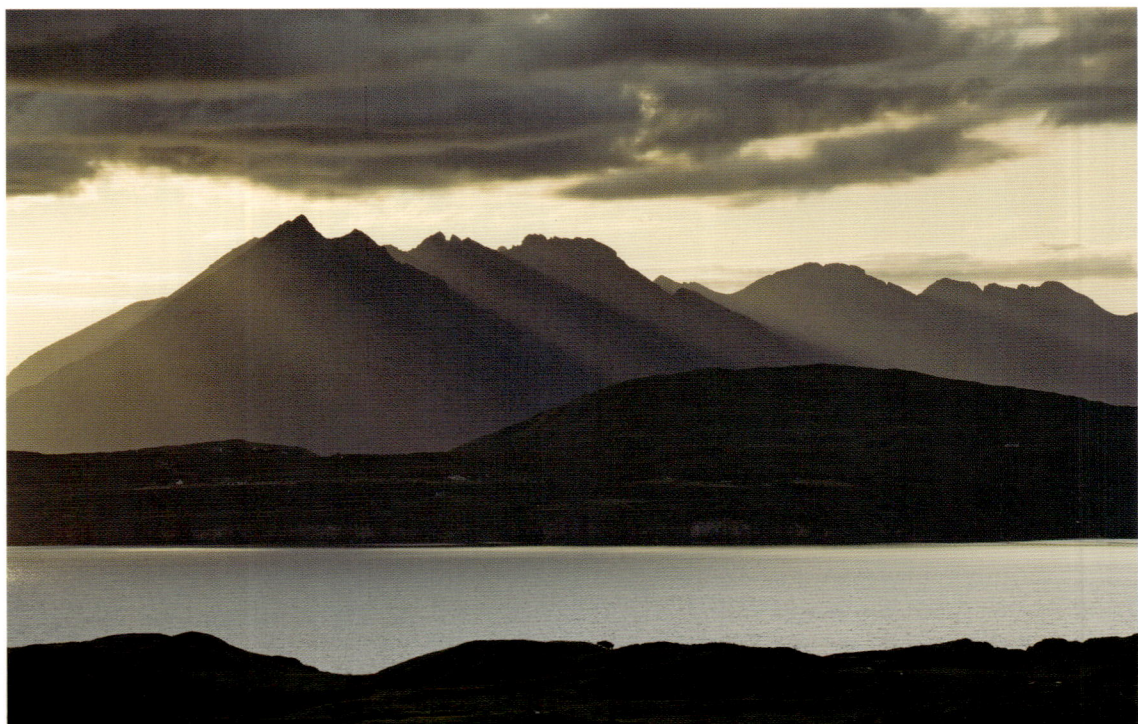

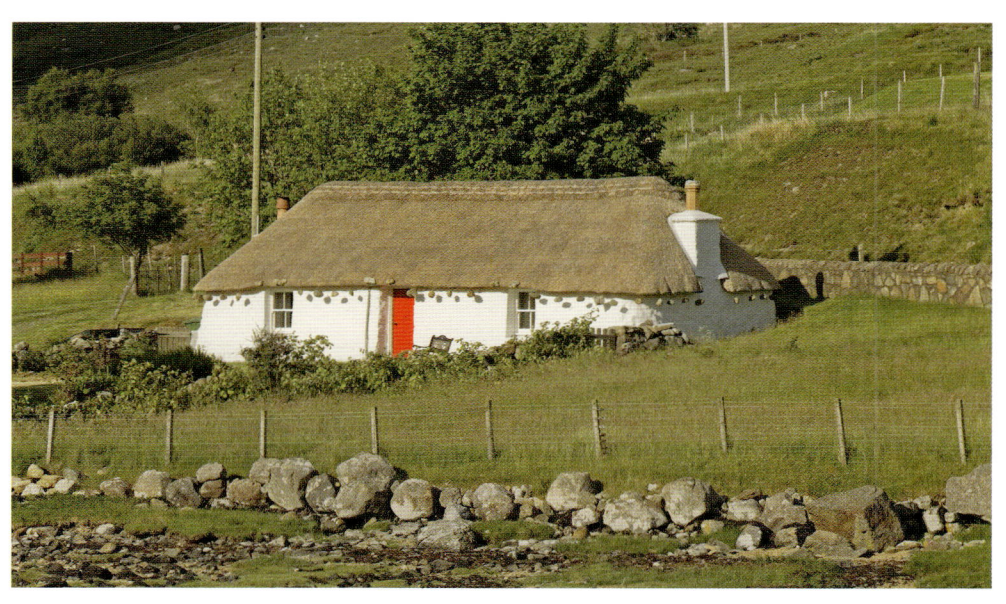

A restored traditional croft house in the small village of LUIB, by the shores of Loch Ainort.

THE CUILLIN HILLS and Strathaird from Tarskavaig, Sleat (left).

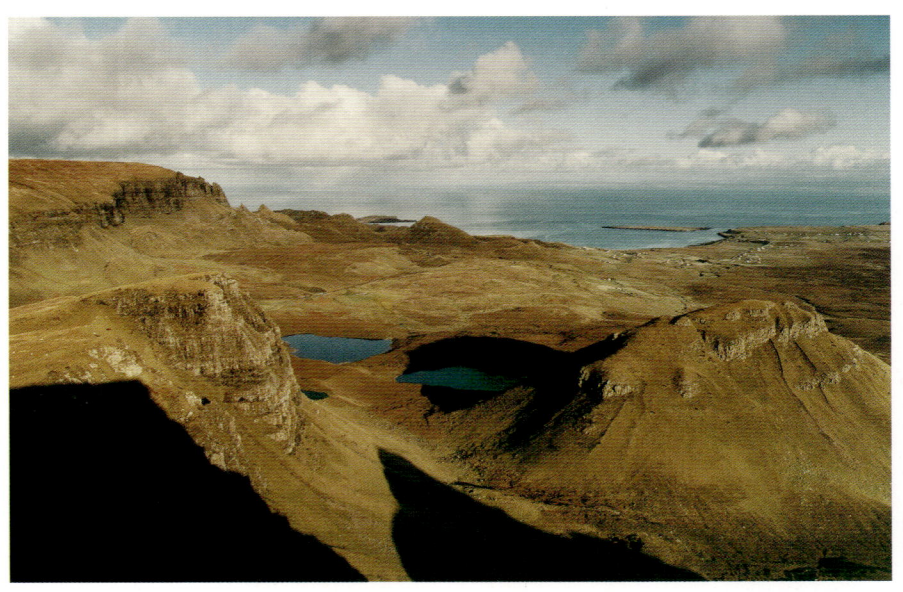

THE TROTTERNISH RIDGE – from the vantage point of Bioda Buidhe (above), with the distinctive landscape of the Quirang unfolding northwards, and Staffin Bay beyond.
THE QUIRANG – towering above Brogaig, Trotternish (right).

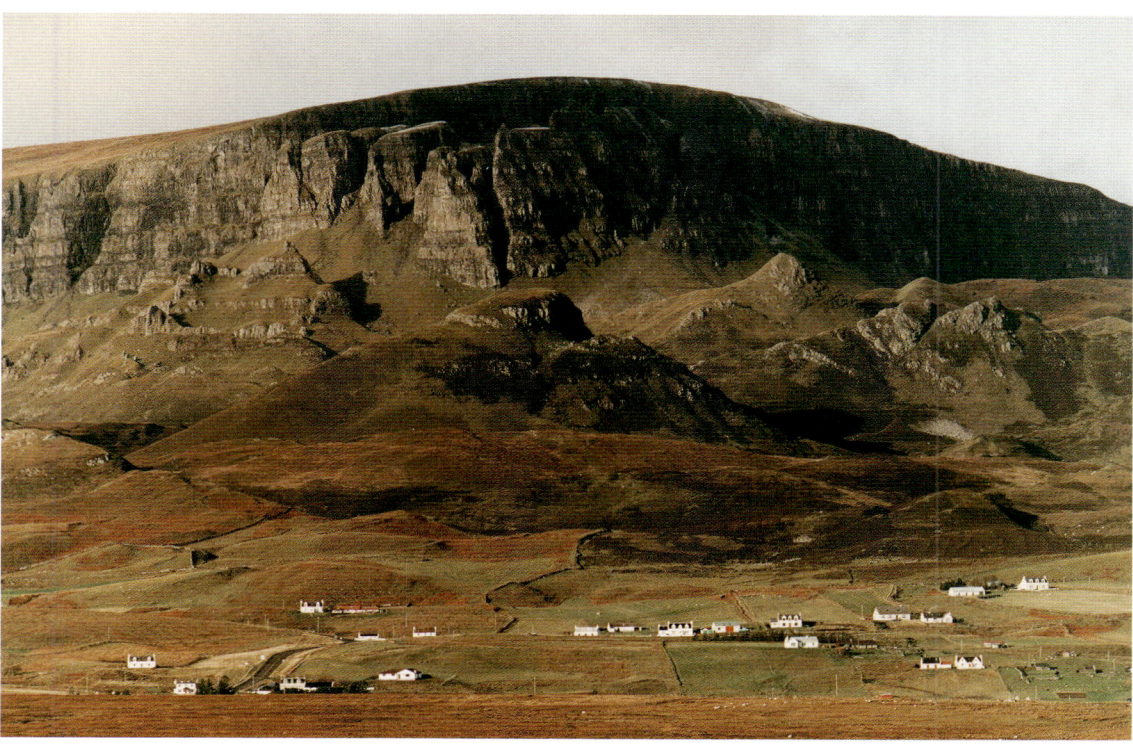

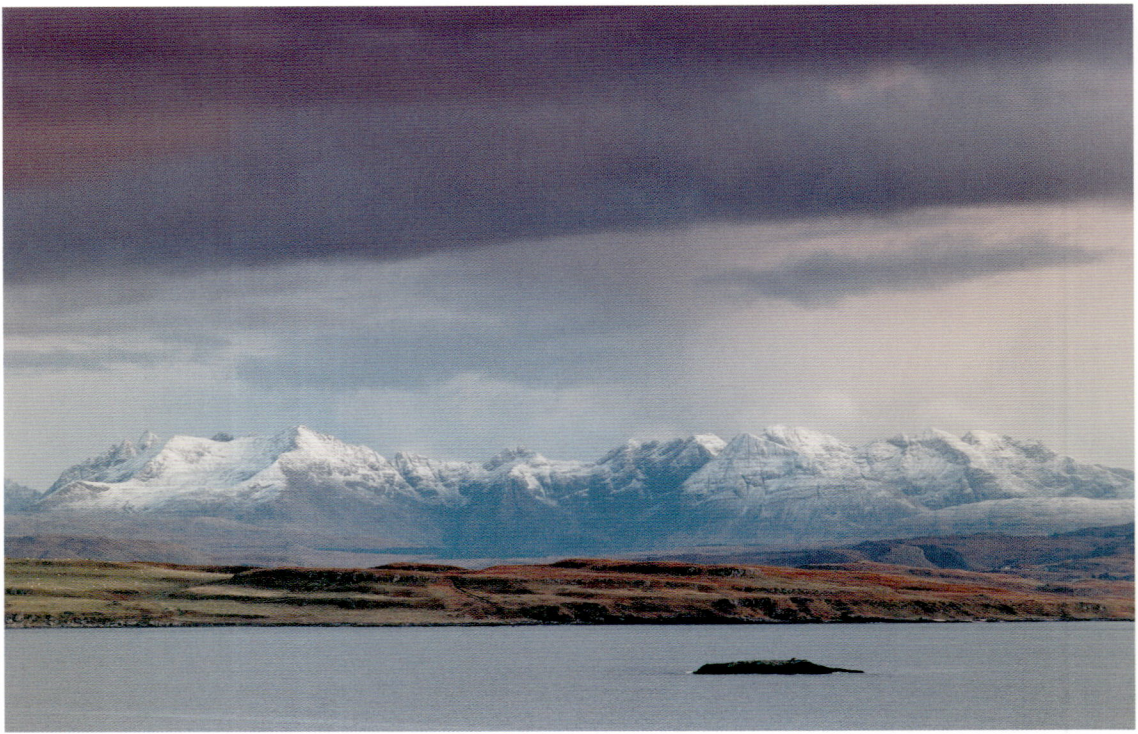

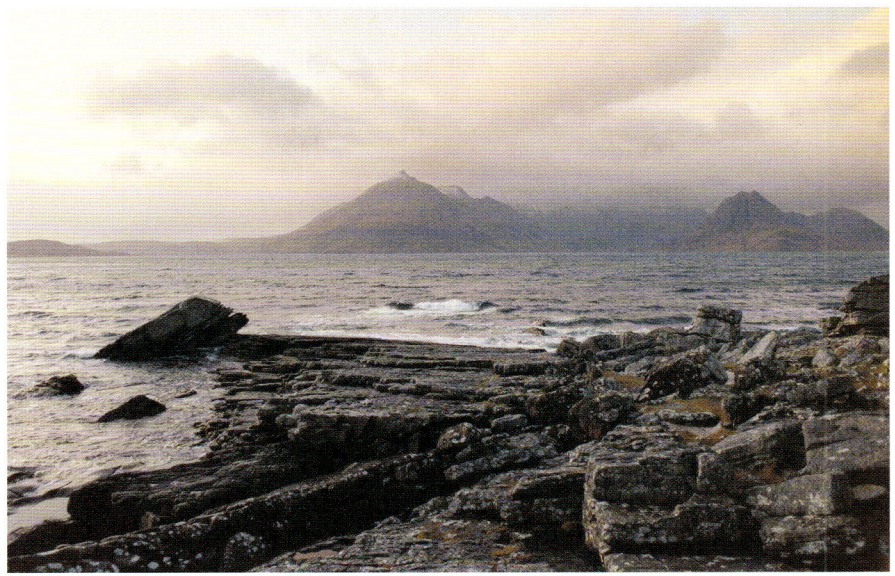

THE CUILLIN HILLS in winter – beyond Loch Bracadale (left) and from Elgol across Loch Scavaig (above). Also known as the 'Black Cuillin' they are composed mainly of rough Gabbro rock, giving climbers a good grip. The highest summit is Sgùrr Alasdair at 3,255 ft (992m).

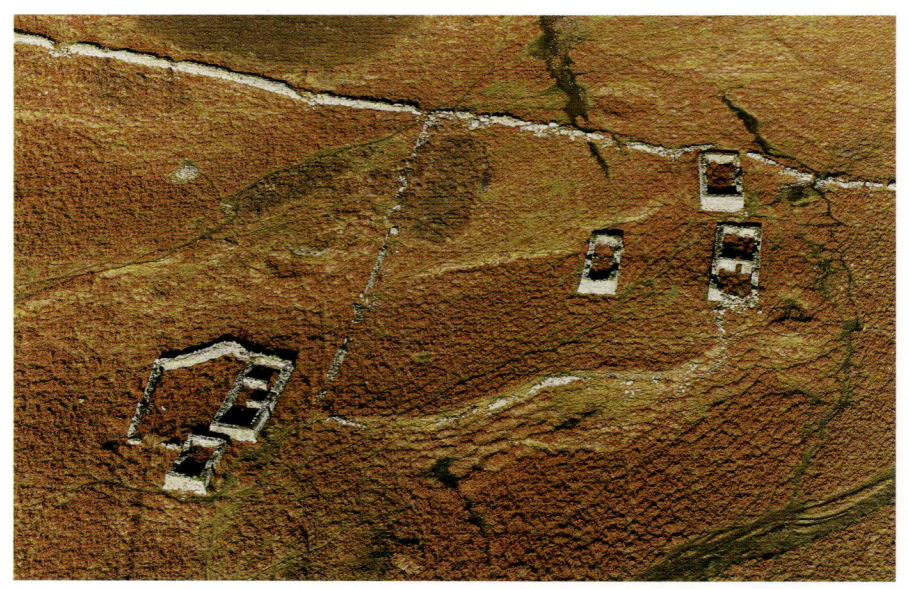

BORERAIG, by Loch Eishort (above) – The township of Boreraig was once a thriving settlement renowned for the legendary MacCrimmon family of bagpipe players, but in 1853 it was forcibly 'cleared', with all the tenants evicted from the land and replaced with sheep.

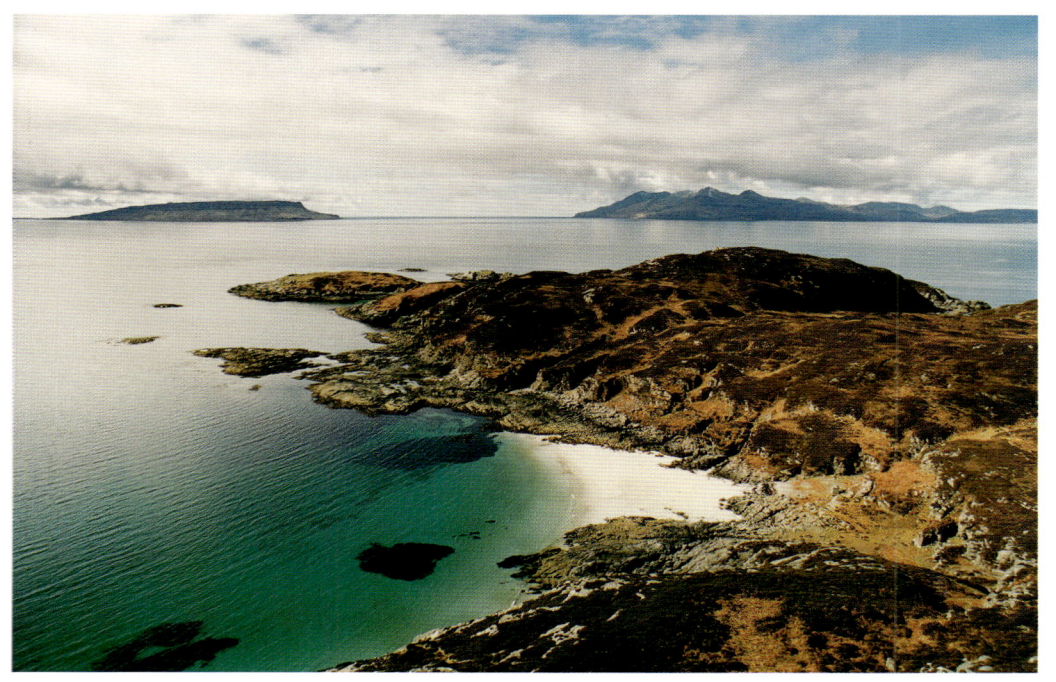

POINT OF SLEAT – with the islands of Eigg and Rùm beyond.

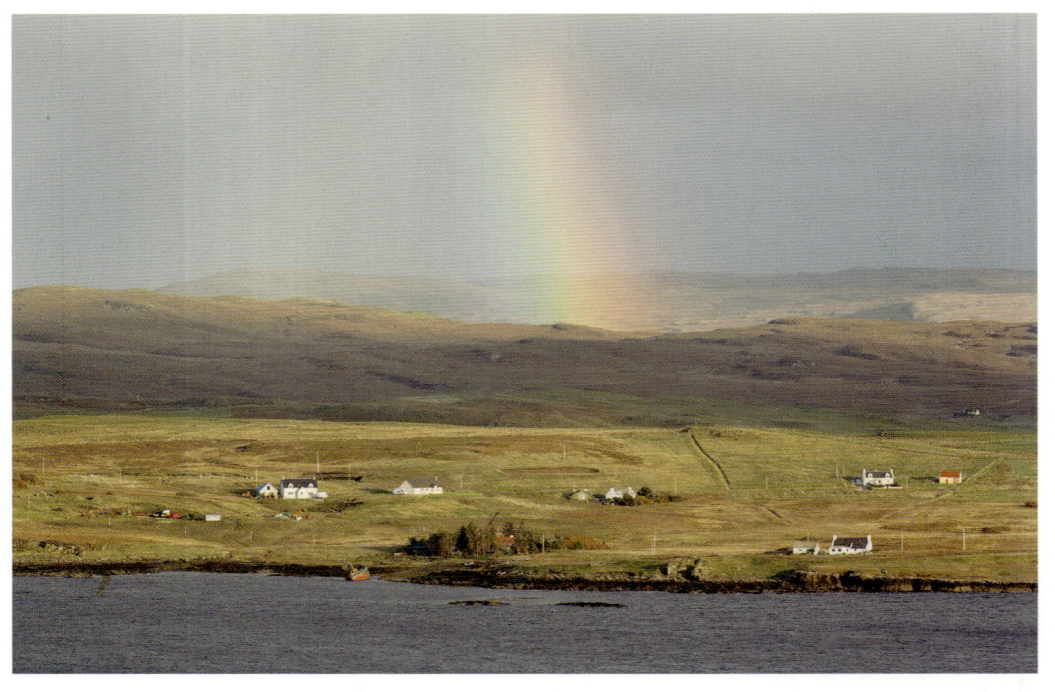

HARLOSH across Loch Vatten (above), and BRUACH NA FRITHE, Cuillin Hills (right).

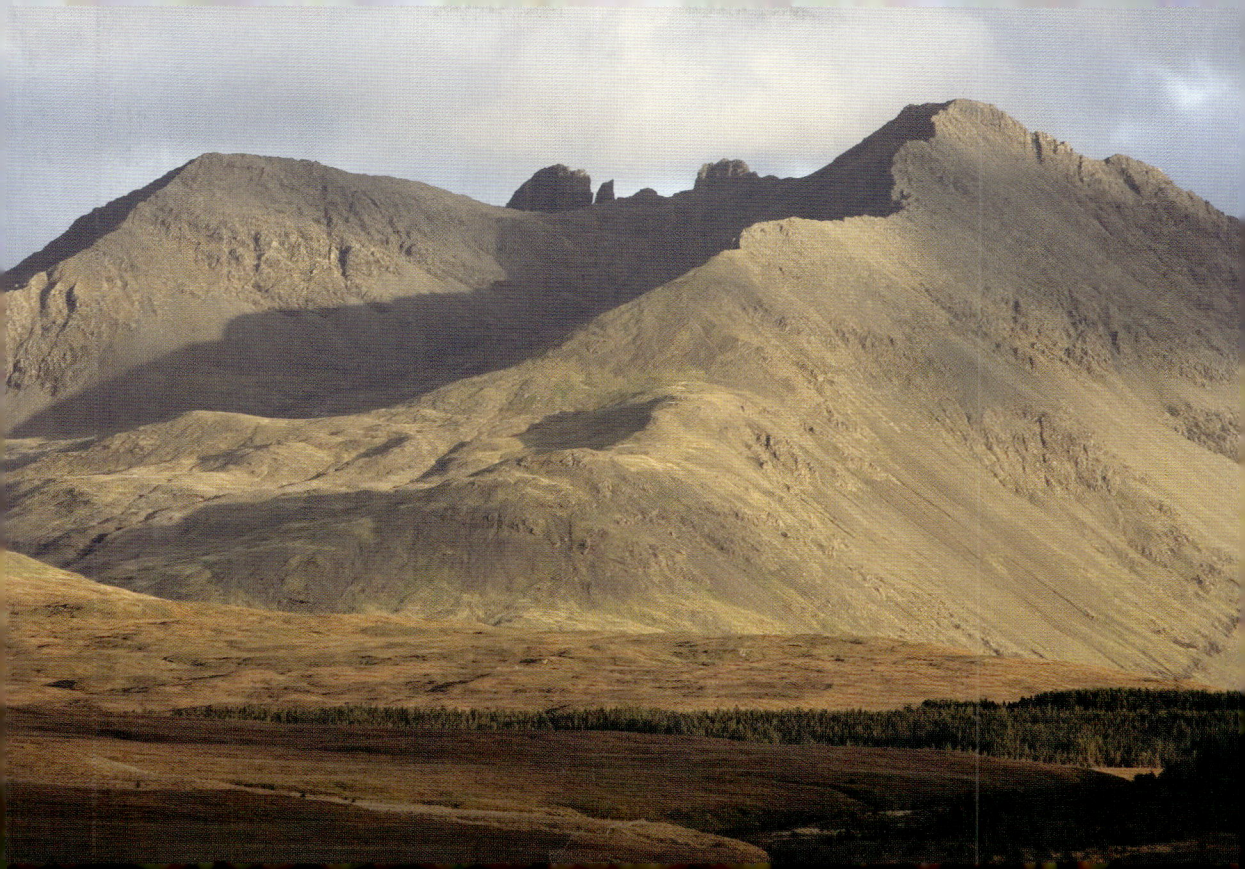

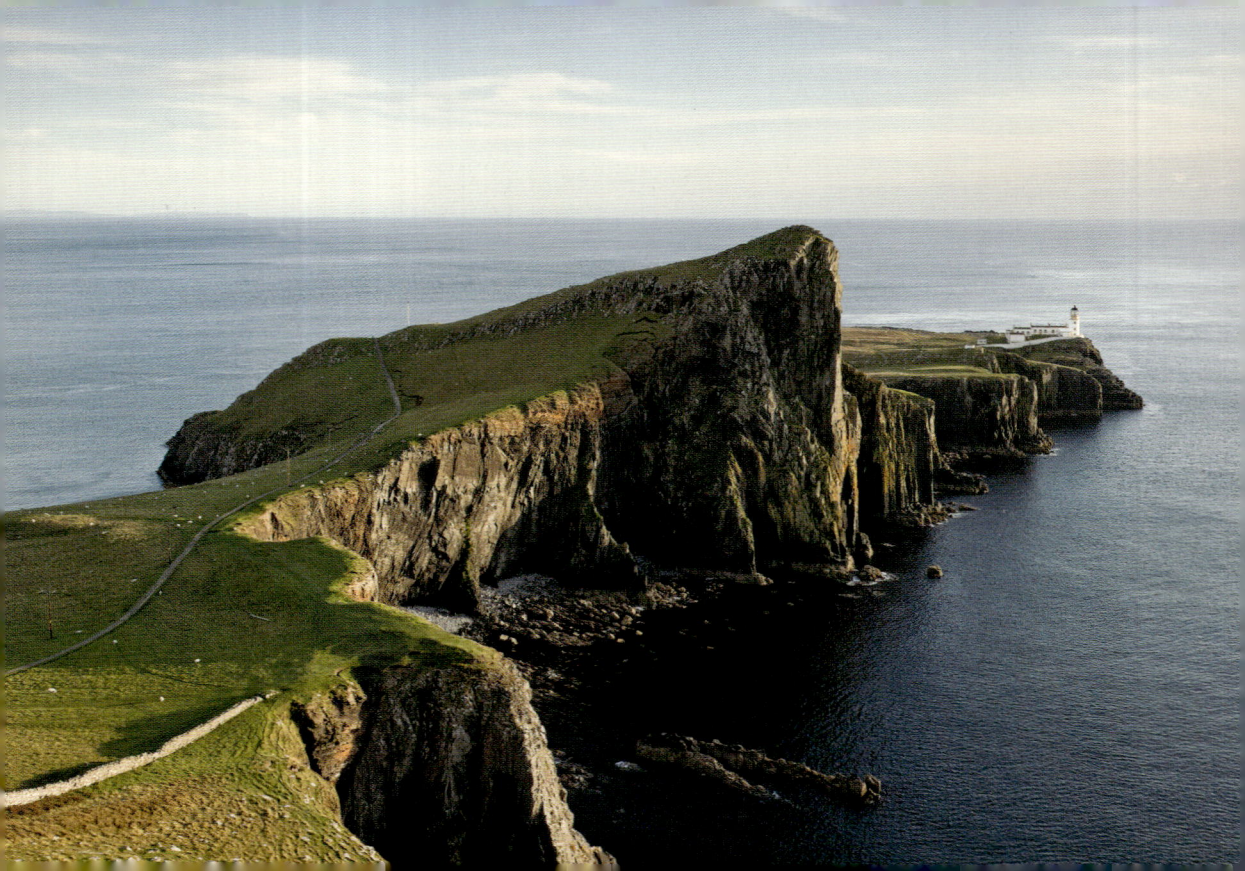

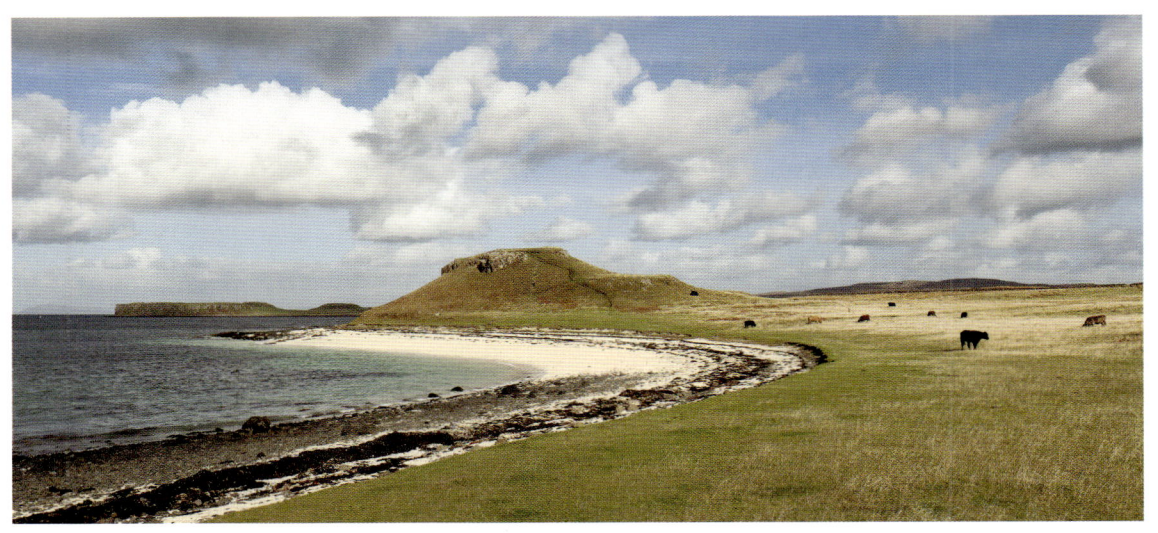

'Coral Beach', CLAIGAN, by Loch Dunvegan – not coral, but dried, calcified sea weed called 'Maerl'.

NEIST POINT, Duirinish (left) – the most westerly point on the Isle Skye.

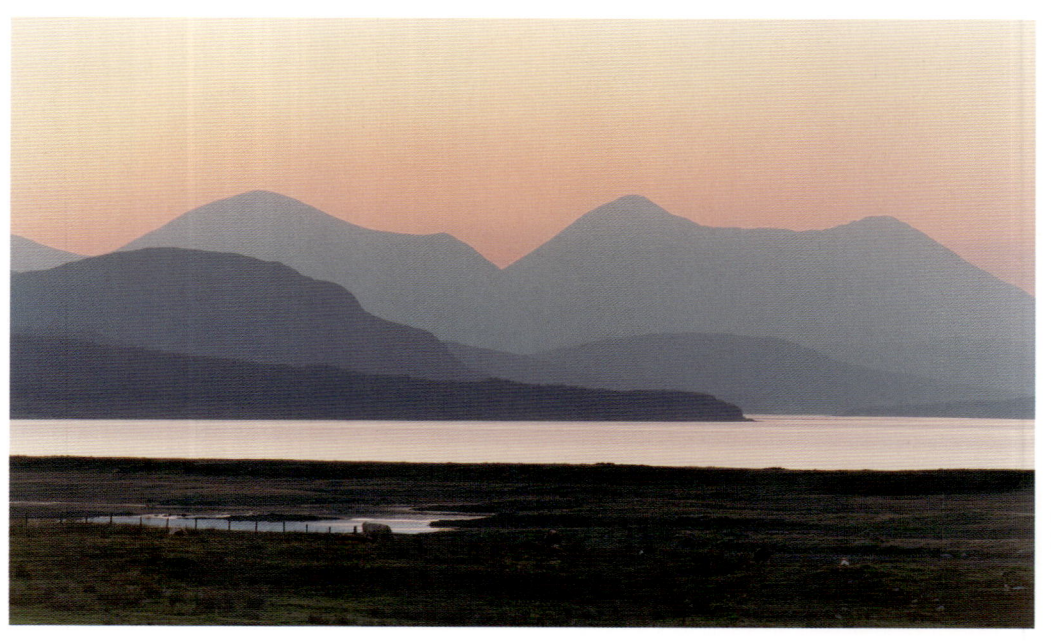

THE RED CUILLIN – As night falls over Broadford Bay in the south of Skye, the more rounded forms of the Red Cuillin, as compared to their Black Cuillin neighbours, can fully be appreciated.

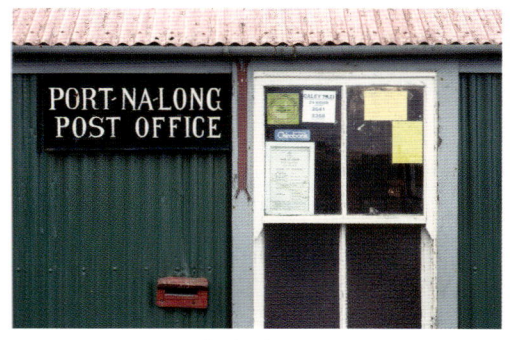
Portnalong.

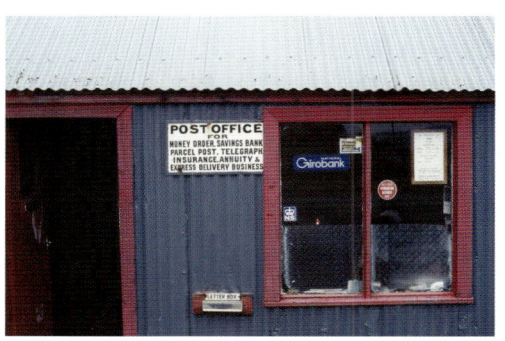
Struan.

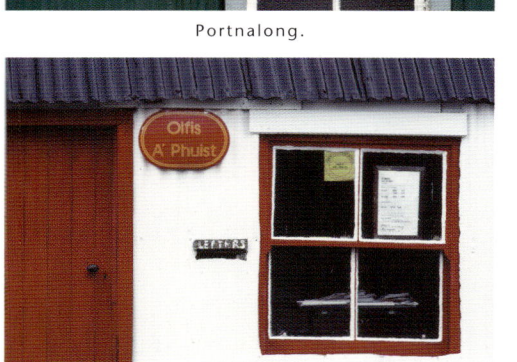
Sconser.

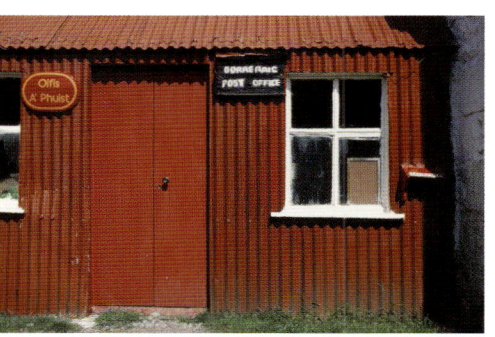
Borreraig.

OLD POST OFFICES.

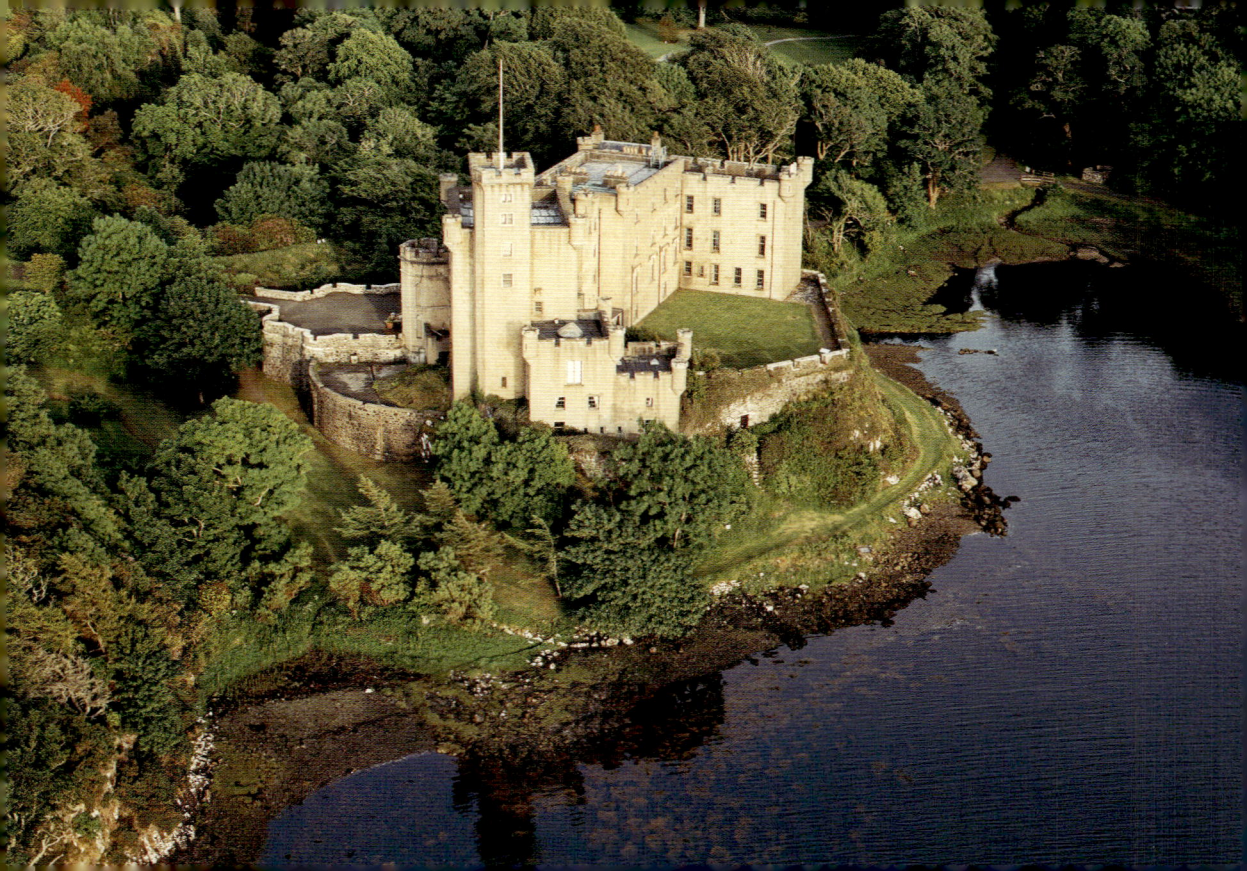

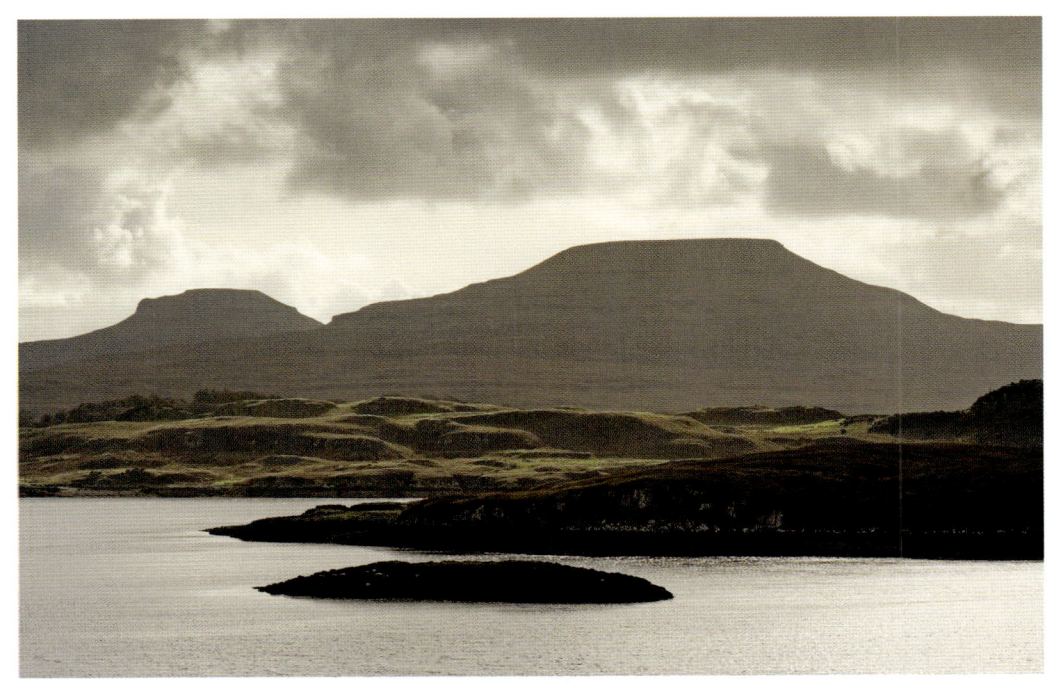

DUNVEGAN CASTLE from the air (left), and MACLEOD'S TABLES across Loch Dunvegan (above).

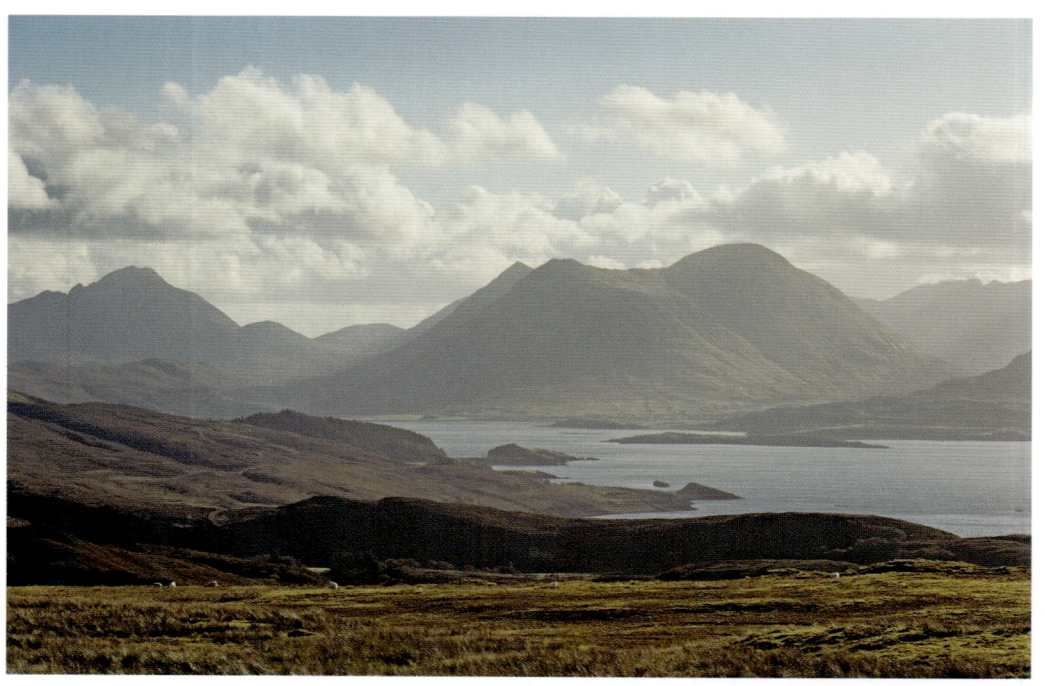

BLÀ BHEINN and GLAMAIG beyond the Narrows of Raasay from Glame, Isle of Raasay.

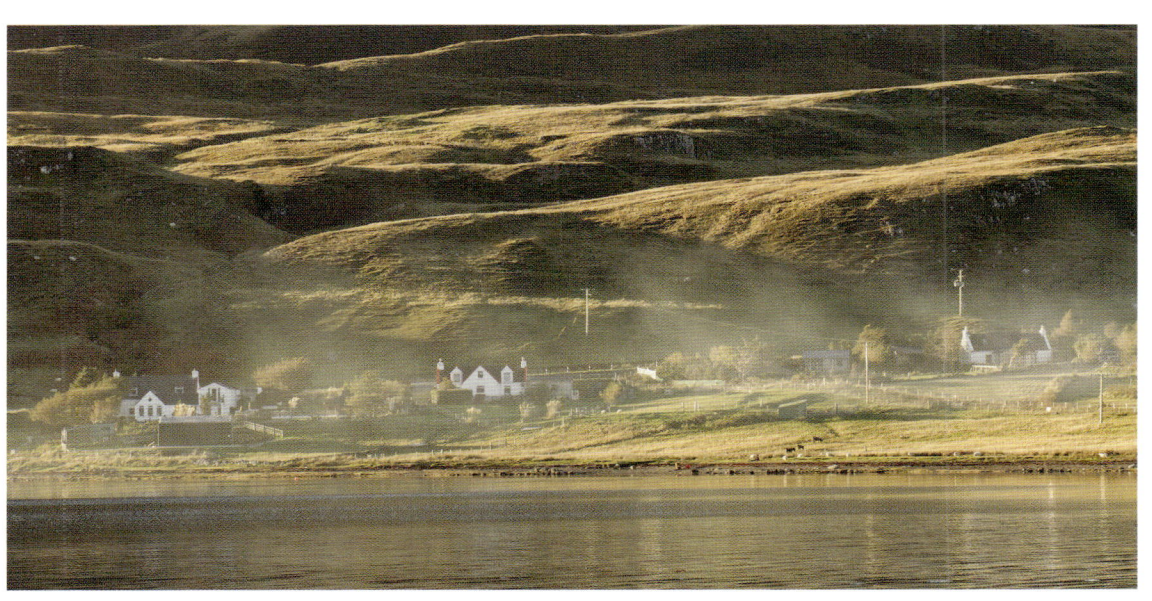

PEINCHORRAN, Loch Sligachan – Skye is the second largest of all the Scottish islands, and as you travel along its 500 mile coastline there are many small, tranquil settlements and townships, such as picturesque Peinchorran by the shores of Loch Sligachan on the east coast.

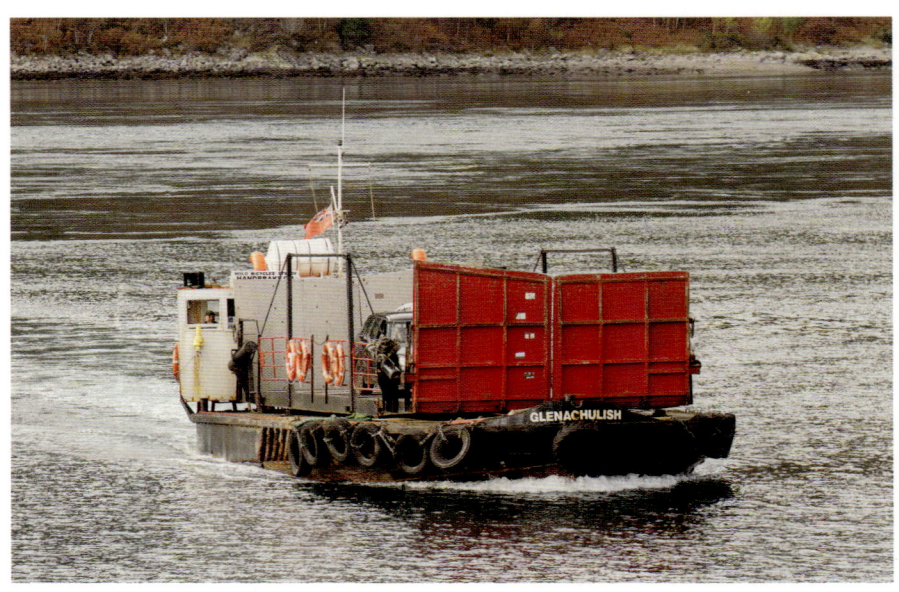

KYLERHEA FERRY – The narrow crossing between Kylerhea on Sleat and Glenelg on the mainland, once popular with cattle drovers in times gone by, maintains a working 'turntable' ferry (above) from Spring to Autumn. THE CUILLIN HILLS across Loch Scavaig, with late winter snow (right).

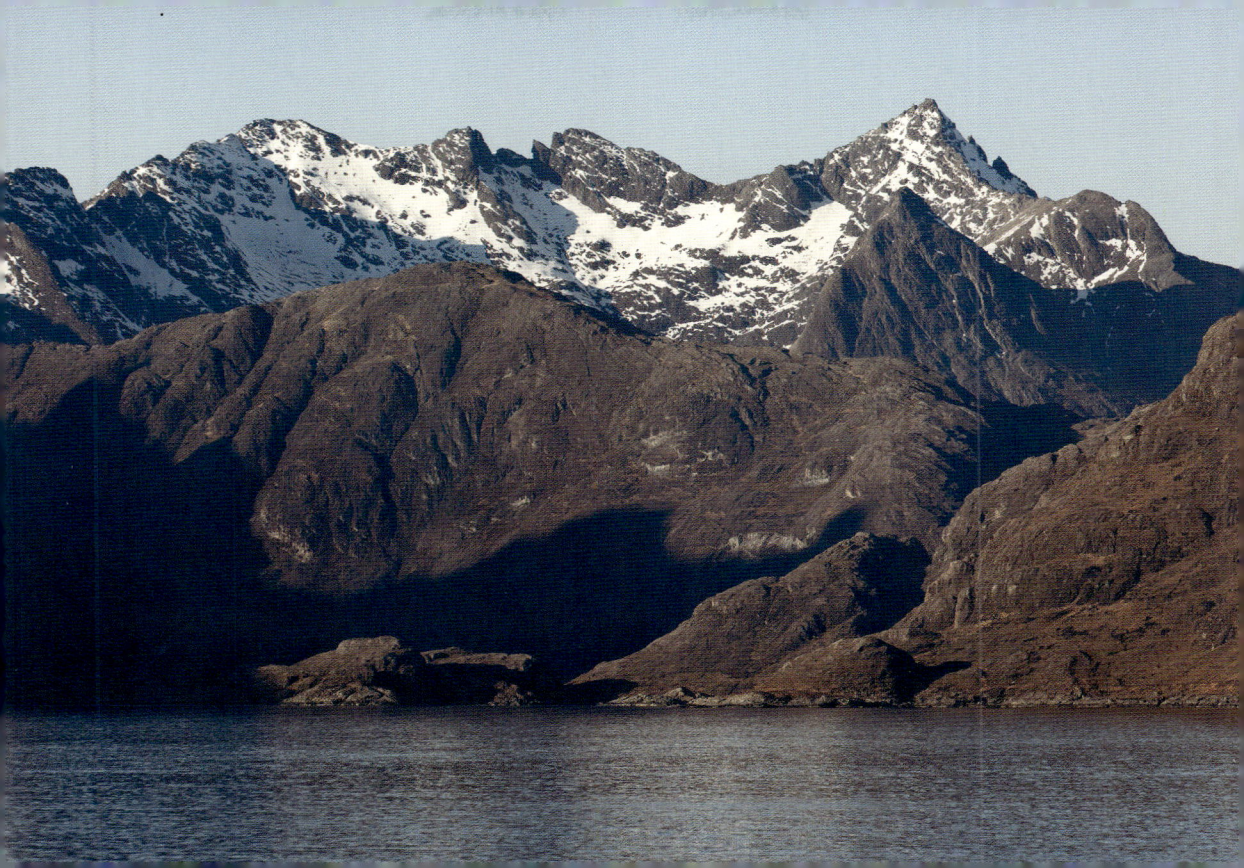

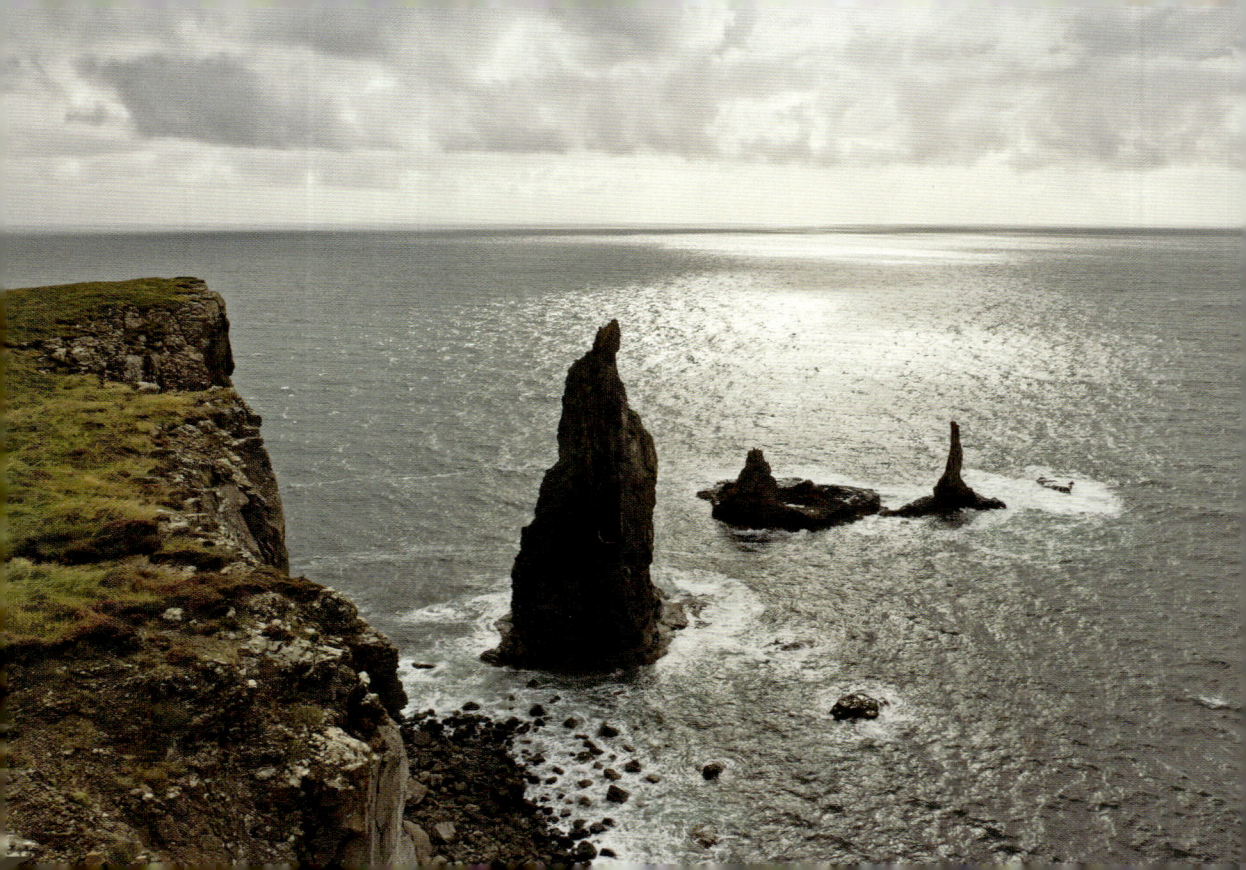

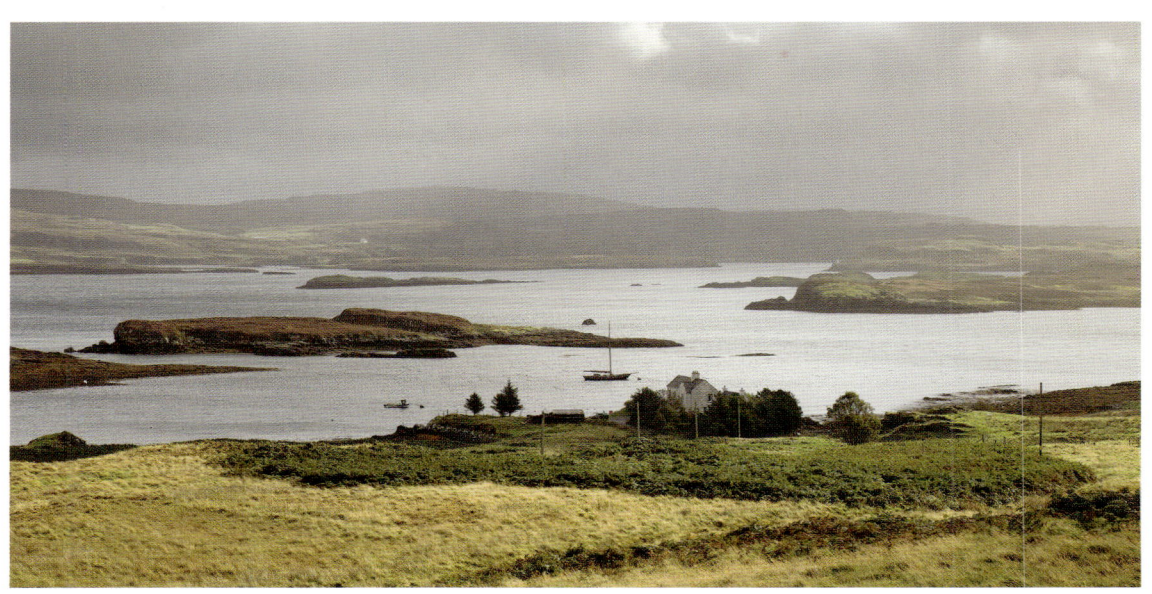

LOCH DUNVEGAN (above) and its plethora of small islands between the Duirinish and Waternish peninsulas. At the southern tip of Duirinish stand three sea stacks known as 'MACLEOD'S MAIDENS' (left), the larger 'mother' stack ensuring that her two 'daughters' never leave her side.

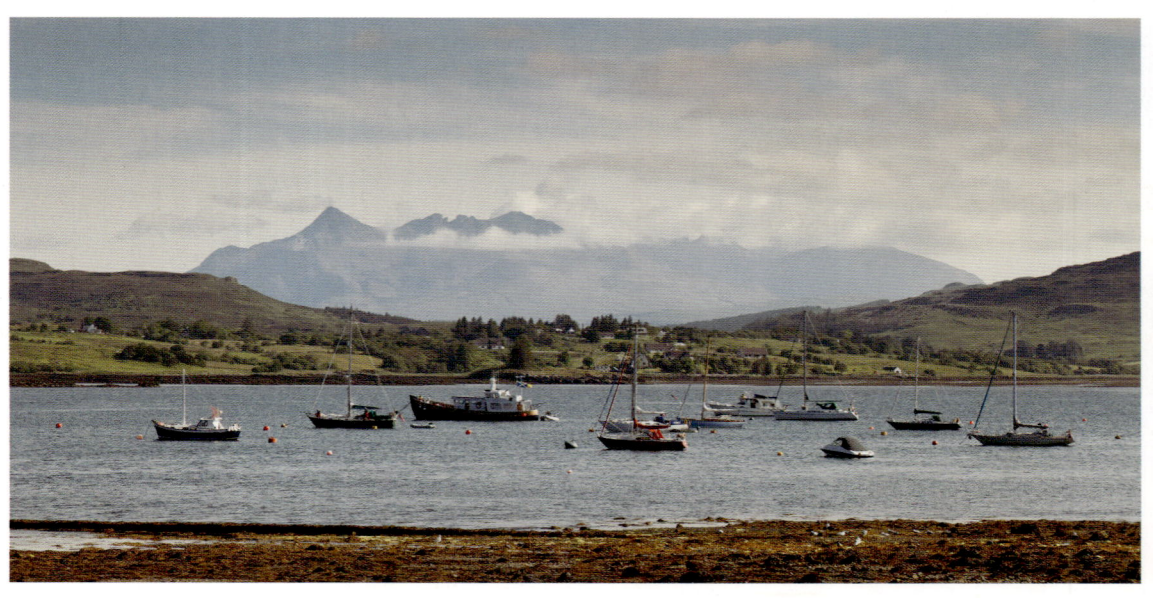

LOCH PORTREE – One of the many things that make the Isle of Skye so special; all shapes and sizes of sea-craft on a tranquil Loch Portree, while in the distance the brooding Cuillin Hills appear on the horizon as if from a different world.

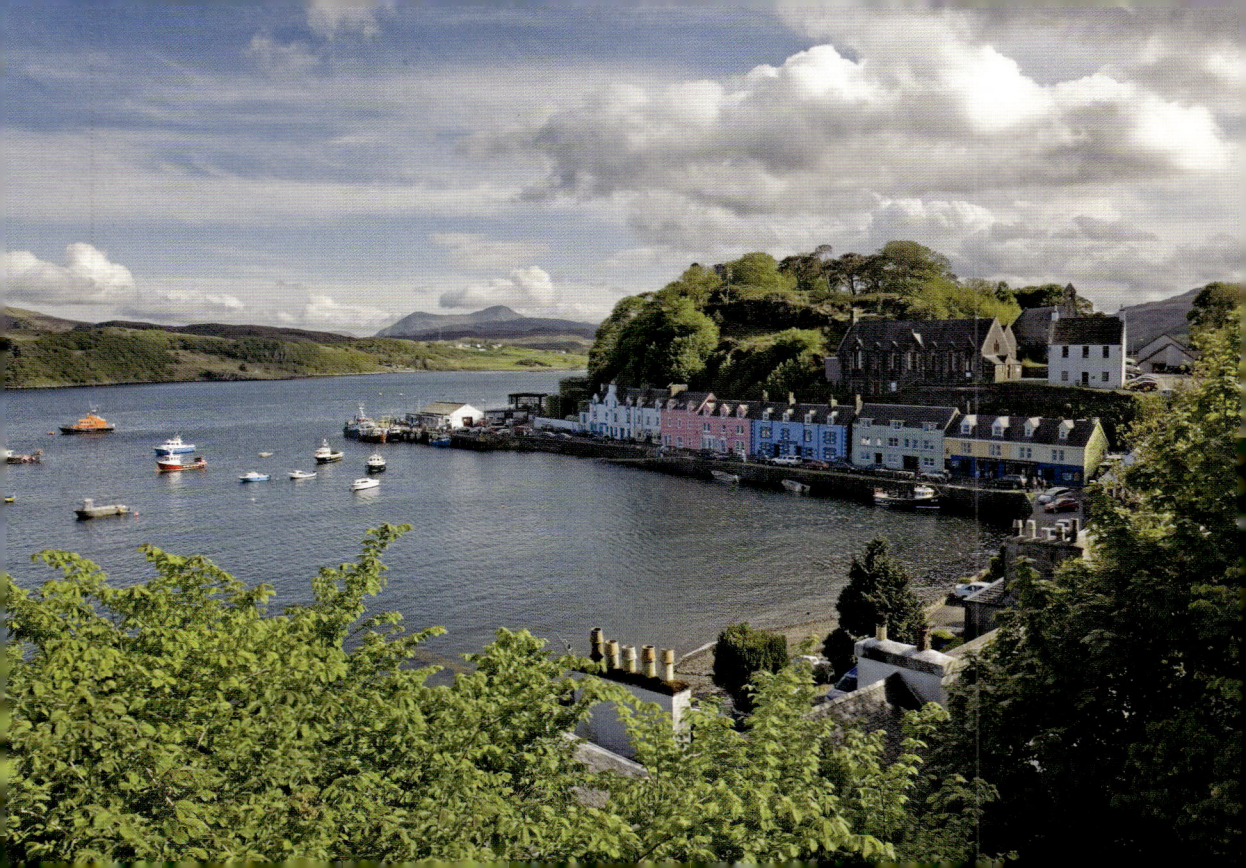

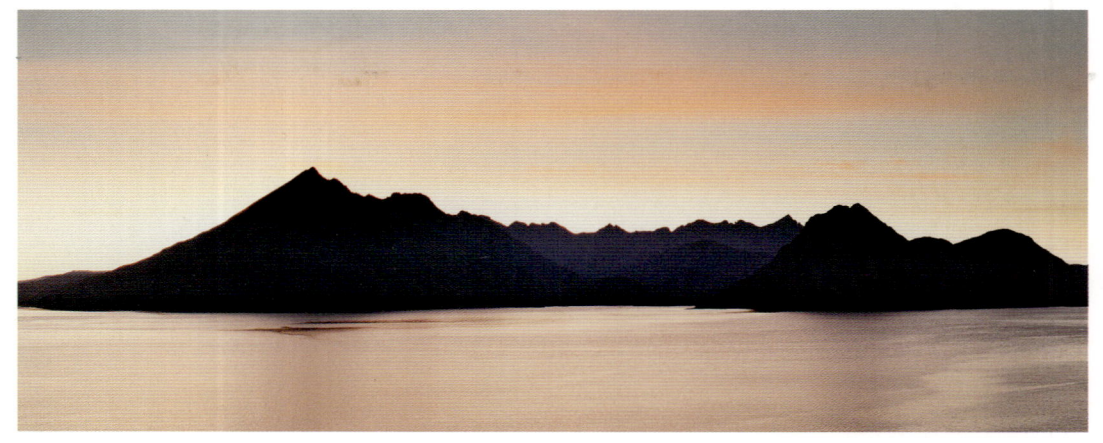

THE MAGIC OF SKYE – The Cuillin Hills from Elgol; one of the most evocative landscapes in Scotland.

This edition published by Colin Baxter Photography, an imprint of Lomond Books Ltd, 12-14 Freskyn Place, Broxburn, EH52 5NF
www.colinbaxter.co.uk

Reprinted 2025
Photographs © Colin Baxter 2025   Text by John Abernethy
Copyright © Colin Baxter Photography 2025   All rights reserved.

No part of this book may be reproduced, stored in a retrieval system or transmitted in any form or by any means without prior written permission of the publishers. A CIP Catalogue record for this book is available from the British Library.

ISBN 978-1-84107-607-2   Printed in China

EU Authorised Representative: Easy Access System Europe, Mustamäe tee 50, 10621 Tallinn, Estonia.   gpsr.requests@easproject.com
www.easproject.com

Page one photograph: NEIST POINT, Duirinish.
Page two photograph: The CUILLIN HILLS beyond Loch Dùghaill.
Front cover photograph: GESTO BAY, Loch Harport & the Cuillin Hills.
Back cover photograph: The ISLE OF SKYE across Inner Sound.